Custom

An Essay on Social Codes

Ferdinand Tönnies

CUSTOM

An Essay on Social Codes

Translated by A. Farrell Borenstein

THE FREE PRESS OF GLENCOE
A DIVISION OF THE CROWELL-COLLIER PUBLISHING COMPANY

This translation is dedicated to
FRANZISKA TÖNNIES HEBERLE

Preface

IN FEW SPHERES of sociological theory is the terminology so chaotic as in the literature on custom. One author might designate as "folkways" what another author terms "usages." What one author calls "custom," another might call "mores," while still a third might speak of "conventions." The present volume must be read with this problem in mind.

Terminological difficulties abound in a translation, since even such closely related languages as German and English do not always contain exactly corresponding terms. The German word "Sitte" has, in our opinion, more of a moral connotation than the English word "custom" which approaches the German "Brauch" (herein translated as "usage"). Therefore, "mores" might constitute a more accurate translation of "Sitte" than would "custom," so far as the generic meaning of the German word is concerned. However, when one speaks of "die gute oder feine Sitte," it is clumsy to render this as the Latin word *mos;* we prefer to speak of "good or genteel custom."

Thus we have chosen the following translations of German terms: "Sitte" is rendered as "custom"; "Brauch" and occasionally "Gebrauch" are translated as "usage," and "Gewohnheit" is rendered as "habit." Terms such as "Kultus" (cult) and "Norm" present no particular problem. Inevitable liberties have been taken in order to preserve what we construe to have been the original intent of the author. For example, the word "Manier" is sometimes translated as "practices," and sometimes as "manners," depending upon the context. The translator has preferred to sacrifice style for accurate meaning, wherever it has been necessary to choose between the two.

A glossary of names appearing throughout this volume which might be unfamiliar to American sociologists is provided in the final portion of this book.

The translator is heavily indebted to Professor Rudolf Heberle and to Franziska Tönnies Heberle for the inestimable assistance and encouragement they so generously gave throughout the preparation of this translation. The fact that *Die Sitte* is now available to English readers is largely owing to their efforts.

A. Farrell Borenstein
LOUISIANA STATE UNIVERSITY

Contents

PREFACE, *by A. Farrell Borenstein*   5

INTRODUCTION, *by R. Heberle*   11

CUSTOM: AN ESSAY ON SOCIAL CODES,
     by Ferdinand Tönnies   29

BIOGRAPHICAL NOTES   147

Introduction

PROPER appreciation of this book will be facilitated if the reader knows how it came to be written and what were the intentions of the author. What we have to say on this subject may also be considered as a small contribution to the history of sociology in Germany.

During the first decade of this century, the later famous philosopher Martin Buber, at that time finding his "way to Hasidism," edited a series of forty monographs on selected phenomena of social life, entitled *Die Gesellschaft*. Among the contributors were Werner Sombart, who wrote the first volume on *Das Proletariat*, Georg Simmel (*Die Religion*), Willy Hellpach (*Die Geistigen Epidemien*), Gustav Landauer (*Die Revolution*), Franz Oppenheimer (*Der Staat*), Ellen Key (*Frauenbewe-*

gung), Joseph Kohler (*Das Recht*) and Ferdinand Tönnies.

Tönnies, though he had not yet received the wide recognition which came to him in the next decade, was already well known among scholars and intellectuals, not only for his *Gemeinschaft und Gesellschaft* but also through many contributions to journals, magazines and newspapers.

Still a professor *extraordinarius* and thus not encumbered with the time-consuming duties of an Ordinarius (a full professor), Tönnies was living in the small town of Eutin, about an hour's ride on the train to Kiel, the seat of his university, and engaged in a prolific literary and scholarly production on a great variety of theoretical as well as practical sociological, political and economic problems. Most of his articles were intended for an educated though not professional public of people interested in fundamental questions of social life or in social problems of the day.

This manner of publication was and still is quite usual among university professors in Germany: some of Max Weber's most important political articles first appeared in the *Frankfurter Zeitung*, and Simmel contributed to many journals.

To this kind of literature belongs also the series

Die Gesellschaft; it tried to reach a broad public rather than only the world of scholars. In his thoughtful preface to the first volume, Buber adopts Simmel's conception of society and sociology: society is action between human beings, sociology the study of the *forms* of these interrelationships, leaving the study of the products (*Gebilde*) of social interaction to other disciplines like ethics, economics, political science, and the study of changes in social life to social history and history of culture.

None of these disciplines can forego a psychological approach without losing contact "with the roots of experienced life." Therefore, Buber says, he selected for his series those among the specialists who were known for their socio-psychological approach.

How far Buber at that time was familiar with Tönnies' work, we do not know. Since he had been introduced to sociology by Georg Simmel, he must have been acquainted with Tönnies' *Gemeinschaft und Gesellschaft* at least in general outline. We do know, through Maurice S. Friedman's monograph, that in the years after World War I Buber adopted Tönnies' theory of history as a basis for his own religious socialism. The image of *Gemeinschaft* as developed by Tönnies must have appealed to Buber, the Hasidic mystic. Beyond these intellectual and spiritual bonds there seems to have been also a congeniality of personalities.

Buber's program for the series, *Die Gesellschaft*, did not provide for the kind of compendium or small handbook-series which presents in concise form the state of knowledge in a given field; his series should rather present new problems and fresh approaches. We must remember that sociology was at that time struggling for recognition as a legitimate field of scholarship and that social psychology was still in its infancy.

The style of Tönnies' book conforms to this program. Far from any textbook organization, it seems to ramble over the whole field of phenomena connected in some way with custom: custom and habit, custom and women, custom in its intricate relations to law and to religion, to morality, ethics and manners, and last but not least to fashion. There are few "illustrations," no footnotes and only sparse references to other authors.

The language, and this we hope will show even in the translation, is not the abstract language of theoretical works in sociology, but easy flowing,

often poetic or at least that of a writer with a strong
sense of poetry. And yet, as we shall see, these
meditations are guided by a quite precise theory
of society and of social norms in particular.

The pivotal idea in Tönnies' essay is the observation that custom, like its individual-psycho-
logical counterpart habit, has three distinct aspects,
the meanings of which are not distinguished in
everyday language. The word custom designates:
1. a fact—an actual way of conduct, 2. a norm—
general prescriptive or prohibitive rule of conduct,
and 3. a will (this is contained in such phrases as:
"custom requires that . . ."). Failure to make these
distinctions, Tönnies claims, has resulted in much
confusion. Tönnies considered his own achievement
was that of having distinguished this third meaning.

In an analysis of habit, he shows how factual regularities of behavior come to assume, for the acting
person, the quality of self-imposed rules. This analysis, extended into the field of collective behavior,
helps to explain how far custom can be regarded
as a manifestation of a common will.

In his earlier work, *Gemeinschaft und Gesellschaft*, Tönnies had already expressed the idea that
social relationships are relations of human wills.
This element of volition distinguishes *social* rela-

tionships from biological and psychic relations. Social relationships, in contrast to the other kinds of inter-human relationships, are real and existing insofar and as long as they are willed by the participating persons. This "willing" may be of a more or less conscious, more or less intentional nature, but it is essential for the mode of existence of social relationships.

The kind of conduct or behavior which a given relationship consists of is prescribed by certain general rules or "norms" of a more or less specific, more or less compulsory nature. Thus the marital relationship is determined in its content by moral, religious, legal and customary rules, all of which together constitute, in Tönnies' way of thinking, the will of this particular relationship.

In this respect there is no essential difference between a social relationship involving two or three persons and a larger association or corporate group. This may sound strange, and in fact it is easier to consider constitutions and by-laws of large groups as expressions of a common will than the often unformulated rules governing a pair or triad relationship. However, if we say "my friendship to X demands that I do this for him" we express ourselves exactly in the way in which Tönnies conceives of social relationships as entities endowed with a will.

The second book of *Gemeinschaft und Gesellschaft* already contained a systematic treatment of social norms. The essay *Die Sitte* thus is an elaboration of one part of this system. The other work of Tönnies in this field is the *Kritik der Öffentlichen Meinung,* a voluminous, partly theoretical, partly historical study of public opinion. Opinion, too, is in Tönnies' view a phenomenon of volition, particularly the opinion of a collective on matters of public concern. And *the* Public Opinion of a society he views as much more than a mere set of ideas or beliefs, for the Public Opinion claims to be true and valid; it is the *right* opinion and demands acceptance and adherence. It has in Tönnies' system the function of a substitute in a Gesellschaft-like order for religiously sanctioned morality in Gemeinschaft-like systems.

Custom is, of course, a form of Gemeinschaft-like social will, of social *Wesenwille* (natural will). It is akin to usage (*Brauch*) and tradition, consequently to traditional or customary law (as opposed to legislative law) and to religious ethics (as contrasted to philosophical or rational ethics). An understanding of custom—its nature and functions—is therefore essential for an understanding of Gemeinschaft-like social order. This essay consequently is important as a complement to the earlier work *Gemeinschaft und Gesellschaft.*

Having thus defined the place of *Die Sitte* in the whole of Tönnies' sociological work, we may now discuss its relation to other treatises on Custom in sociological literature. A comprehensive survey is of course not feasible within the scope of this introduction. However, for our purpose—that is, in order to place Tönnies' study in perspective—it is sufficient to consider comparable works of a general or theoretical nature.

Sumner's *Folkways* had been published about two or three years before *Die Sitte;* there is no evidence that Tönnies knew it nor does Sumner seem to have known *Gemeinschaft und Gesellschaft,* although he was quite familiar with a wide range of German literature.

Tönnies, like Sumner, was influenced by Spencer's sociology and there are most likely some other common sources. It seems, however, that Tönnies depended less on anthropological information than Sumner and that he relied more on juristic literature, particularly on Jhering whom Sumner did not mention. Some parts of Tönnies' essay read like a debate with Jhering. No doubt Tönnies felt he could improve on the great jurist's theories.

The two books are so different in character that a fair comparison is difficult. Sumner's *Folkways* is a broad and comprehensive treatise on every possible aspect of the folkways and mores, illustrated by ample anthropological and historical references; Tönnies' book is a compactly written short essay of a more theoretical nature and intends to be no more than that.

Sumner, as the subtitle of his book indicates, used the word "folkways" as a generic term for the specific "codes of conduct" referred to as "usages, manners, customs, mores and morals." Folkways are the basic patterns of social conduct from which develop rules of greater or lesser moral significance and consequently greater and lesser force to regulate social conduct. The degree of enforceability is one of the criteria of distinction.

Tönnies also assumes that all social norms are evolved from a basic sense of order, derived from habit; some kind of rules are found in any group, even if no name is given to them. The term "usage" comes closest to the concept of this primary norm of order.

There is one fundamental difference between Tönnies and Sumner: the latter regards folkways as merely *de facto* ways of behavior, whereas Tönnies recognizes the norm character in all habit and usages. He would consider even those folkways that seem to lack enforcement sanctions as obligatory rules of conduct, the violation of which to the actor as well as to others appears as a disturbance of the social order. The violation may not have grave consequences, but that does not detract from its being a breach of rules.

In Tönnies' system—as it was developed later— the theory of social norms is an essential complement to the theory of "social entities" (relationships, collectives, and corporate groups), because all social relationships in Tönnies' system are viewed as *"geltende Dinge"*—i.e., as things having validity, and it is this quality which makes them *real* for the individuals involved or concerned.

In explaining this idea Tönnies liked to draw the analogy to ghosts (or gods) which *"are* real" to the people who believe in them; social relationships and groups are "real" insofar as those who form them recognize them as realities and act accordingly. This involves obedience to norms. This way of thinking may be hard to follow for sociologists trained in a behavioristically oriented theory and unable to see the difference between patterns of behavior and rules of conduct, or, to put it differently, who identify "expected behavior" with *"norm."*

As we pointed out at the beginning, this identification of pattern and norm of conduct is partly due to the failure of language to distinguish, as Tönnies does, between the three aspects of custom (and folkways).

Social action is more than mere inter-action; it is inter-action guided by general rules, rules that are binding in different degrees, to be sure, but nevertheless demanding respect and compliance. In our opinion, one of Tönnies' major contributions to sociological theory is his clear recognition of this element of obligation that is contained even in those patterns of conduct which, like mere usages, seem to lack any sanction.

Even Max Weber regards "Sitte" as *de facto* regularities of social action, not attributing to it any norm-character. For Weber, the rules of conduct are either "convention" or "law"; both arise out of *Sitte* or may become *Sitte* if the kind of behavior which they demand becomes entirely habitual (traditional). *"Konvention"* for Weber means rules of conduct valid within a particular "social environment" i.e., within social circles or social collectives (*Samtschaften*)—to use Tönnies' terms.

Violation of convention may be penalized by "informal" action of group members, such as boycott—but no specially designated enforcement apparatus goes into action as in the enforcement of legal norms. It may be contended, then, that Weber's concept of *Sitte* corresponds to Sumner's "folkways," while his *"Konvention"* corresponds to *"mores."*

Further, Tönnies has traced the *moral* or *ethical* element in custom, which, although very diluted and hardly noticed, is contained even in simple "folkways" or usages. The moral element in usages can be experienced when, having deviated from habitual ways of acting, we (and others) feel that "something was not quite in order"—we may not be very concerned about it, but we feel slightly disturbed. The maintaining of an order of conduct, in the sense of regularity, tends to become a value in itself.

Contrary to Sumner who believed that folkways were norms of a lower order essentially different from the norms of higher order—the mores—Tönnies shows that all norms form a continuum. There are many transitions between the various categories of norms; customs (*Sitten*) may become *usages,* or they may become *law.*

Even the principles of morality are firmly grounded in custom (*Sitte*) except for the moral (or a-moral) doctrines propagated by innovators, be they religious prophets or philosophers or charismatic political leaders (a concept which Tönnies did not use) who, if successful, could create new customs and new law.

We have now touched upon the question of how norms change. Tönnies saw a fundamental difference in this respect between the norms of community and the norms of society. While the former, as part of a sacred tradition, tend to change only slowly, the latter, which are regarded as means to ends, may be changed quickly and frequently in order to comply with changing conditions of society or with the demands of powerful special interests. Thus "legislative law" may be radically changed or repealed by "a single stroke of the legislators' pen" (as a great jurist once complained).

Usages, custom, customary law and religious ethics tend to be resistant to change; the "manners" of "good society" (or of the "smart set") are subject to frequent and rapid change, and so are of course the norms which prescribe what to wear at given occasions—not to speak of the everchanging norms of "fashion." Public opinion, too, contains elements of fluidity and may condemn tomorrow what it sanctions and accepts today.

Sumner failed to see these fundamental differences between norm-categories and consequently repeated *ad nauseam* the doctrine that folkways and mores could not be changed willfully but change only imperceptibly and gradually in the course of time. This position of Sumner's amounted to a nearly complete rejection of social reform by legislation—an attitude obviously inherited from Spencer. Curiously, there is also in Sumner a sort of diluted historical materialism: his doctrine, he said, "is antagonistic to the view that philosophy and ethics furnish active and determining forces in society and history . . ."

According to Sumner, the folkways develop as men meet needs; if long enough practiced and found effective for the welfare of the group, they become *mores* and "thence are produced faiths, ideas, doctrines, religions, and philosophy, according to the stage of civilization and the fashions of reflection and generalization."

This really primitive scheme leads Sumner to com-

mit such flagrant blunders as his "ultimate explanation of the rise of humanitarianism" through the
"increased power over nature by the acquisition of
new land . . ."—"when men ceased to crowd on
each other, they were willing to adopt ideas and
institutions which made the competition of life easy
and kindly" (p. 39, sec. 45). Obviously this is a
gross distortion of historical facts.

Tönnies, although he was strongly influenced by
Marx, never advanced such ideas of crass material-
istic determinism. He was too aware of the power
of ideas, especially of religious beliefs, as an "independent variable."

Nor did Tönnies hold Sumner's contempt for the
common people. While Sumner stated that "the
great mass of any society lives a purely instinctive
life just like animals" (p. 45), Tönnies saw the source
of custom among the "people"—the peasants, the
artisans, the "folk" as contrasted to the more ration-
ally minded upper strata. The people, in holding
on to customs, are doing so by no means "instinc-
tively" but from conviction and often because old
custom seems to serve their interest better than
new legislative acts.

The wealthy, the politically powerful, the educated and enlightened strata are the innovators, the makers of legislative law, the creators of fashion, the sponsors of civilizational progress and therefore —although often unwillingly—the destroyers of custom. Their achievements, the capitalistic economy, the modern state, and modern science, are all opposed to tradition and therefore to custom.

An age of fashion, of legislative law and of civilizational innovation succeeds and overpowers an age of custom and traditionalistic culture. And yet, in the concluding section, Tönnies expresses the belief and the hope that changes in the economic system toward an "economy of use" could eventually lead to a "more stable, quieter, healthier" way of life and that this would offer a chance for the development of a value-rational (to use Max Weber's term) code of ethics along with a philosophical religion.

In other words, Tönnies gives expression to his often restated belief in a regeneration of Western society and culture through a new kind of *Gemein-schaft* based upon an organically developed combination of state- and cooperative-socialism. He was therefore radically opposed to Russian Communism (Bolshevism) which destroyed all genuine *Gemein-*

schaft or its survivals. Likewise he objected passionately to the Nationalsocialists'—the Nazis'—attempt to create a "Volksgemeinschaft" by compulsion.

RUDOLF HEBERLE

Louisiana State University
Baton Rouge, Louisiana

Custom:
An Essay on Social Codes

THE word *Sitte* is a synonym for habit and usage, for the transmitted and for tradition, but also for fashion, practices, and the like. Those words which designate habit tend to be interpreted as if their content were essentially unequivocal. Actually, speech (unconcerned with more profound distinctions) blends the most diverse meanings. I find that habit, to examine this most general expression, has a threefold meaning, namely:

1. The meaning of a simple fact of an objective nature. In this sense, we speak of the habit of rising early, of going for a walk at a certain hour, or of taking an afternoon nap. We mean nothing more

than that one is "used to" doing so, he does it regularly, it belongs to his way of life. But it is easily seen that this meaning shades over into

2. The meaning of a rule, a norm, which a person establishes for himself. Thus we may say "he has made it a habit" and, in the same sense, "he has made it a rule for himself" or even a "law," and we mean that the habit operates like a law or like a "precept." One follows it; one regards the habit as a binding command, a subjective creation which, however, has objective form and validity. The precept is applied to behavior. A commandment itself can be imagined as prescriptive, demanding, commanding. Thus habit also becomes

3. Expressive of volition or of a will. This is the least noted meaning, but actually the most noteworthy. But if habit is the will of a man, it can only be his *own* (personal) will. In this sense, the terms which refer to habit as "second nature" and to men as "creatures of habit" are significant. It is, indeed, a psychic disposition which sets into motion and pervades a certain action. And this is will in its most pronounced aspect, as a resolution or a "firm" intention. *Will* ever has its roots in "wishing." It is so closely related to it that in speech both words are used synonymously. Thus

we say "will" where we can only mean "wish." But wishes originate in sentiments, in elementary relations through which the organic creature reacts to his surroundings, positively with pleasure and negatively with aversion, accepting and rejecting, desiring and detesting. Habituation—that is, habituation conceived of as a characteristic of an individual—also belongs to sentiment.

As a rule, what one is accustomed to becomes thereby quite "bearable"; he even *loves* and is attached to most of it. He wants to preserve and keep it all the more naturally, the more it is dear and valuable to him for other reasons. Habit not only alleviates suffering, trouble and labor; it also compels one to certain conduct and action. It is equivalent to need. To be sure, habit dulls one against enjoyment. It modifies pleasant as well as unpleasant sensations. It is a condition of equilibrium of the soul. Established habits imperceptibly change into the instinctive. What we do habitually we do "involuntarily" just as we involuntarily make gestures, movements of welcome and of repulsion which have never been taught to us but in which we are skilled "by nature." They spring from the instinct of self-preservation and from emotions which stem from it.

However, what we are accustomed to do, we have had to learn and practice first. It is precisely the practice, the frequent repetition, which eventuates in our finally doing it as if by itself—reflexively, quickly and easily, as the tight-rope dancer walks on the rope because he is accustomed to do so. Thus habit or usage is partly the reason why a man is able to do something at all, and partly why he achieves something with relatively small effort or attention. But being accustomed to doing something is not only the basis for our being *able* to do it, but also for our actually *doing* it. It works in the way of a stimulus and, as has been said before, as a need.

The "power of habit" has often been depicted, frequently praised, and often lamented. As with a magic force, it draws the drunkard or gambler at a certain hour toward his accustomed place in the club or inn. His itching, vexatious desires (all the more vexatious the more they have become habitual) are appeased when he holds the accustomed mug or accustomed "book of four kings" in his hands. But the principle is identical to that which facilitates the art of the tightrope walker or the pianist. Practice eases the will; it paves its path. It intensifies our wishes as it strengthens muscles and nerves. It overcomes resistance, and friction, and precisely *because* of practice a "passion" may become a dominant, indeed a forceful despot.

As habit is essential to vice, it is essential to virtue as well. Aristotle has strongly emphasized this point. Habit not only strengthens our good inclinations, encouraging and challenging us in our struggle against the base, but it supports those motives which are weak but beneficial for the individual or for his society. Above all it hardens us, the spirit, like the flesh, enabling people to resist and to bear hardship, and making them willing to do so. Every educator knows the high value of habit in this regard. But for all this, we do not find that the element of will is recognized in habit.

What is "will" as we understand it here? Not inclination *per se*—as stated above, habit is also inclination—but inclination insofar as it has assumed the form of thought. For only man is capable of willing, and human will is always thought. Thus habit, insofar as it is will, is immersed in thought so to speak, and it presents itself as the thought "I will,"—that is, as a free *decision*. Nevertheless, the "annoying" habit can be the deciding power, the decisive one, in spite of that consciousness of freedom.

Habit propels the alcoholic even if he normally believes that he acts freely, believes that he could "do otherwise" and undoubtedly would be declared "responsible" by any psychiatrist or judge. Indeed it is his action that he wills, but not the deliberation and the decision. The latter are perhaps still combined with and influenced by the opinion that the body needs "refreshment" or "relaxation," perhaps even with the firm purpose of being moderate this time. The real and essential will is not what lies on the surface of consciousness. These are only the busy servants and messengers who pave his way while the sovereign sits unseen in his coach. The real and essential will is habit—that is, will which has become lord and master through practice.

Opinions are, as a rule, dependent upon habit, and conditioned and prompted by it. But they can certainly also extricate themselves from habit and elevate themselves above it. They do so when they become principles or convictions. As such they assume a firmness which can break habit and overcome it. The firmness of "faiths," in the familiar religious sense as a certain trust, is a primitive form of *firm* will. Thus, while habit and opinion are generally rather compatible with one another, there also lies the germ of conflict and struggle. Thought tends to become the ruling element in the mind, and in this fashion man becomes more human.

But I am not going to discuss here the manner in which habit extends further and deeper into will. I only mention this in order to lead to the concept of custom as essentially *social*-psychological, in analogy to the basically *individual*-psychological concept of habit. The words "usage" and "custom" embrace the threefold meaning of mere fact, of norm, and of the will which sets the norm. As I see it, the discussions of custom have not, up to now, recognized this threefold meaning, and thus have not been able to distinguish them from each other. I have almost exclusively held to the second meaning, to custom as a norm.

The famous jurist, Rudolf von Jhering, has devoted an intensive study to custom in the second volume of his work, *Der Zweck im Recht*. Indeed, this present book contains repeated references to Jhering's study. Jhering, too, understands "habit" as a social phenomenon, and conceives of it as the mere actuality of established general behavior. He defines "custom," on the other hand, as a *socially binding* validation of habit which was combined with it. Language, he asserts, discerned the command of custom but not the command of habit.

But it so happens that the idiom "habit" refers to the individual, and "custom" to the commonwealth, the people, and that commandments are always understood to be social. Furthermore, with reference to the plural—"customs"—Jhering thinks that this strict distinction is not observed. Among the customs of people about which travelogues inform us, "customs" may be obligatory as well as non-obligatory, "mere usages, the observance of which is optional—thus, in our way of speaking, not instances of custom but of habit."

Jhering's contribution in making this distinction is valuable, but he is here as elsewhere in error about the idiom. Even the singular, "custom," is continually used to indicate a mere matter-of-fact practice, in which there is nothing obligatory implied. For example, we say it is the custom in England to pay by check, or "in the Middle Ages it was frequently the custom for men and women to bathe together," or "the use of the bicycle has generally become a custom."

In these cases, no one would ever dream of maintaining that any urgency existed because of the custom. On the contrary, it is commonplace—when this is the meaning—to say "custom wants," "custom demands," and even Jhering uses these ways of expression. Hence we may also say, in the second of the above-quoted examples, "custom permits that the sexes bathe together." We perceive immediately that the word has an entirely different meaning here. That meaning is one of authority or of a powerful will, for only he who has "a say about something" can give permission.

But if we talk of customs in the obligatory sense as of facts, then this meaning evidently lies between mere actual practice and authority. We talk of actual norms, of valid rules, of customs as if they were laws. Wundt, to whom we are indebted for an astute discussion of custom, has put this most striking meaning literally at the base of his theory. For example, he thinks that "sordid custom" remains custom as long as the character of a binding norm is at all attached to it.

I maintain, on the other hand, that the sociologist must in the first place study and isolate custom as a highly important form of *social will*. He must perceive and analyze social will in analogy to individual will. The same meaning which "will" in the ordinary individual sense has for individual men, "social will" has for every community or society, whether they represent themselves merely as loose relations or as associations and organizations.

And what does the meaning of "social will" involve? I have indicated the answer to this in my discussion of habit, and here make the generalization that social will is the general will that serves to order and regulate individual will. Every common will can be understood as expressing a "thou shalt" and, insofar as an individual or an association of individuals addresses this "thou shalt" to itself, we perceive its autonomy and freedom.

A necessary consequence of this, then, is that the individual at least tries to maintain his will against opposing dispositions and opinions, and the association against opposing individuals, however such resistance may be expressed; and that they have the effect of urgency, of "bringing pressure to bear" —and this is essentially independent of what means are available. At least in the social sense, means vary from persuasion through praise and disgrace to actual force and penalty, the latter also being expressed as physical constraint. "Custom turns into the most obstinate, overwhelming power." (Schmoller.)

If we impute a will to custom, thus personifying it, this is not a precise way of speaking. Custom cannot be imagined without people who want what custom wants. Who are these people? Colloquial language answers this question when it refers to custom as "folkways." The "folk" is represented as the creator of custom. Who is this "folk"? The "folk" is a mysterious being, not easy to comprehend. It is almost easier to *feel* what the "folk" is, than to conceptualize it. For we do not really understand it if, following the (German) dictionaries, we define it as "the totality of mass of people; the totality of the so-called lower classes; the totality of people of one language."

The word "folk" must be given still another, more particular meaning. I daresay that it connotes not only the living, but also the dead, and those to be born. Indeed, it especially connotes the combination and the unity of these three levels—a community wherein the dead by far outnumber the living, since they are composed of limitless numbers of generations. No one can presume statistically to comprehend the individuals who, in this sense, be-

"Folk"

long to a "folk" because they have once belonged
to it; for what has been will always more easily be
regarded as existing than what will be.

We believe that we behold something infinite
and unlimited, and a touch of the sublime drifts
toward us from the past. Only this meaning explains
why we presume to know what "folk" is, and yet
can barely describe what we mean when speaking
of folk stories, folk tales, and folklore. In more recent times the words "folk spirit" and "folk soul"
have also developed from this same meaning. "Folk
custom" as we shall understand it here belongs to
the latter just as "will" otherwise belongs to the
soul and to the spirit.

If we speak of the custom of a country, we no
doubt think more of what is actually done, practiced, or performed, than of the will which lies
behind it and at its basis. Thus one says, as in
Faust: this is not the usage of the land. For we
use the term "usage" almost exclusively when we
think of mere facts. "Usage" in the singular case
can hardly be given the meaning of a legislative
will. In the German language a distinction is made
between *Gebrauch* (usage) and *Brauch,* which approaches the meaning of custom. *Brauch* was formerly used by German students' fraternities to

USAGE
(TIE TO LAWS)

ETIQUETTE

indicate what is now called *Komment,* or the written rules of conduct.

All historical books and travelogues tell us of the manifold and diverse customs and usages in various countries and at different ages. A philosophical inquiry, confronted with this diversity and confusion, must raise the question: Where does the one-ness, the common-ness and the essential nature of custom lie, which must be comprehended in all this diversity? And from this question the following problem arises: Can the essential substance of custom as a configuration of the general will be developed from its manifestations? For form and content together comprise the essence of a thing which we understand as the object of a concept. The following essay will principally be concerned with the solution of this problem.

*   *   *

According to its form, custom as general will is essentially concerned with itself. Every will is directed toward self-preservation, the will of the people to the life of the people, and hence to the *welfare* of the people. We note that the word "well" recalls "will." But, as we said before, the will of the people is more a *general* will in distinction from and in contrast to individual will, insofar as it wants to order, regulate, and establish. In its essence, the will of the people is also a necessary and logical will in distinction from and in contrast to fortuitous will, which is determined by affect, passion, moods and whims. I have introduced the term *Wesenwille* as the will that corresponds to this concept, and I am retaining it although it has as yet found almost no acceptance. In this concept, reason and will are one. Habit is an expression of individual *Wesenwille* and custom an expression of social *Wesenwille*.

Just as habit plays a decisive role in individual life, as man calls habit "his nurse" and accuses it of being a tyrant, so we know that custom enjoys a superabundant power in the life of peoples and nations. We know that where law and the executive power of the state compete with custom, custom often proves itself to be superior, and that it is always held to be older and more sacred.

We can thus understand custom as a sort of legislative will, but we know that it is not—like the latter—formulated through a resolution, be it of an individual ruler or an assembly. Rather it is formed through habit and out of practice: it is based on tradition. Therefore, it points toward the past. The fact that our forefathers held it "this way" and practiced it, will always be given as the decisive reason why we, too, should hold it this way and follow the same practice.

In this sense the Romans coined the expression *"mores majorum"*—the customs of ancestors—and a German song says, "Be true to your forefathers' sacred customs." The main idea is not that our ancestors wanted or demanded it, but that it is required because they have done it. It is based on the common reasoning that we must and we want to act as our forefathers have acted; we must and we want to follow their example and their precedents.

This reasoning leads easily to the further argument, "for that is useful and wholesome for us" and "since our elders knew what is right, their wisdom is greater than ours" and "the way they have done things has been tried out and proven as immemorial usage, as the way in which tradition has maintained itself."

Thus understood, acquiescence to custom and fostering of custom are only special cases of obedience and imitation through which the young and disciples follow their parents and masters and learn from them. Indeed, this is one of the most general laws of social life: it is the essence of tradition in life and in all arts. If we inquire into the origin of a custom, we are referred back to the infinite series of past generations. "It is a very ancient custom," "it has been so forever," "since time immemorial . . ."

For that very reason it seems to be natural and necessary and as good as what one does according to natural desires, and as good as the language which a people know and use as their own. But one does not always stop here. Out of the obscure past a lawgiver will occasionally be given as the author of a custom, as the man who first inaugurated its use and commanded it. This lawgiver must, then, have indeed been a holy man, one godlike, since he possessed this wisdom and because our fore-fathers obeyed him. Perhaps he himself was a god or the son of a god; at all events a superhuman figure, swathed in the flowing vestments of legend.

But this consideration does not alter the general rule that the ancestral practices are regarded as the essential basis for *duty* to which the living are bound, and that in this way fostering custom rests in the reverence with which the living venerate the dead. This reverence is again a special case of reverence which children show their parents and the young show the old. Such reverence is usually regarded as their duty. Of itself, this reverence is based not on custom, but actually on nature, on "natural law"—that is, on a tacit understanding about what has to be.

This understanding results from the actual state of affairs as an inference and a claim. It is "self-evident" and therefore necessary. The word reverence (*Ehrfurcht*) is in German composed of honor (*Ehre*) and fear (*Furcht*). It is natural that the weak man "honors" the strong and the child "honors" the adult. To honor means to admire, to regard as great and powerful. At the same time to honor someone means to regard him as good—that is, as in some manner benevolent and kind toward one, and to look up to him pleadingly or gratefully.

It is just as natural that the weak fear the strong, and the child fears his parents. And reverence is based on the fact that the feared one is not shunned and detested as an enemy, but is esteemed and honored as a friend, as help and comfort, as lord and master. Or, reverence is in essence that indeterminte "holy" awe which is induced by a wonderful power, by the spirit which emanates from a venerable countenance and manifests itself in a mysterious and solemn way.

To manifest and uphold reverence for elders is

part of custom wherever it is strong, profound and powerful, since reverence is at the core of custom. The Spartans, whom one can call the people of custom *par excellence,* are a model. And it is true of all old civilizations—as still today of the Chinese —that the parents enjoy special care, and indeed sanctification, through custom. The Mosaic law "Honor thy father and thy mother" was at least as highly valued by the Greeks and the Romans.

But if honor and care of the mother appeared to be primary and most natural, then honoring the father was the more bidden by custom. It is still more independent of natural sentiments when custom wills that the old *per se* receive testimonies of reverence, that they be fed and nursed, and that one take their advice and their admonitions to heart.

The usages of certain primitive races seem to stand in sharp contrast to this when they expose or kill their old and, indeed, even bury their own parents alive. Yet even this can be inspired by love and by pity. Under the circumstances of harsh necessity and a nomadic existence, it may function as an act of kindness and good will. Indeed it is narrated that often the old demand this as their privilege and are grateful for it. Perhaps the custom of India that the old men "go into the woods"

in order to lead a meditative and hermit-like existence is a residue and a descendant of that ancient
barbarianism.

The characteristics of peasant brutality from
Christian eras are almost more repulsive. Custom
apparently permitted that the young married couple
mistreat the "retiring parents" and let them go
hungry. Such atrocities are hardly recorded of the
pagans of antiquity. Solon is believed to have said
he would set no punishment for parricide, because
he did not hold such a crime to be even conceiv-
able. And Aristophanes allows one who has killed
his father to go into the kingdom of birds because
he thinks that there the custom of biting and chok-
ing the father prevails. The birds answer him that
such a thing is unheard of among them. They
deem it to be a peculiarly human custom, and they
point to the storks as an example of caring for
parents since they had been cared for by them
when young.

The value and significance of custom often con-
sist in replacing an earlier, more natural (because
cruder) practice and in restraining it. Therefore
in the consciousness of a people it is related to the
proud idea of distinguishing themselves as noble
and civilized before the barbarians among whom

the more wicked custom is practiced.

Quite naturally, reverence is transferred to the unseen spirits, the spirits of the dead who are imagined as continuously living and acting, to whom one owes the food and drink which they have enjoyed while living, and who—unless they have their fixed and tended place of rest—"go about" and become dangerous, inclined to do harm. Custom commands calming, reconciling and cheering them even if they, as spirits, must ultimately be satisfied with the fragrance of flowers.

The cult of the dead, of fathers and mothers in particular, develops into the cult of ancestors. The worship of heroes and gods stems from ancestor worship. They are the ancestors of the chiefs or of the whole tribe. Finally, the highest god is even the father of all men and especially of all gods, the "creator" of heaven and earth. The cult of the dead is therefore a custom of very particular significance. One might call it the custom of customs, and the custom which at the same time lies at the root of religion, as a custom which rises above custom, links itself with it, and sanctions it.

Certainly religion is not custom in every sense. Partly it is also regarded as natural, as self-understood, like the *obsequium* or the obedience which children owe their parents: because the gods exist they must be revered (as "ours"). Partly the special reverence is traced to their own deeds and accomplishments, to special communications and "revelations," and hence to the gods' own will—as, indeed, the dead claim sacrifices as their right.

In fact, according to the old Aryan view which is still found among contemporary Indians and which was familiar to the Greeks, the chief purpose of marriage is to beget an heir-proper who will bring offerings to his deceased father in a valid form— that is, in a manner sanctioned by custom. For custom does not only determine that a cult be practiced, but also the How, the manner and form of rites and ceremonies. Whatever is done should be performed correctly, for only thus will it have the desired effect.

But how is it correct? As it always occurred, as one has learned it. And how has one learned it? In any manner in which the natural sentiments, feelings of servility, of humility and diffidence, all of them expressions of reverence, are expressed strongly and distinctly through the performance.

In addition, feelings of grief and sorrow over the loss of the deceased, together with admiration for his good qualities and his power, gratitude for his heroic deeds and his favors—sentiments expressed in hymns of praise and gratitude—must also be thus expressed.

But the manner in which these feelings are expressed may have primarily been dependent upon countless, relatively accidental factors, particularly upon different endowments of tribes and peoples, and upon their differing sensitivity and taste. Imitation of neighbors and aliens plays a role here, and the whole variety of superstitions in magic contributes toward this.

These various factors have partly never been conscious. Partly they fall into oblivion. But everywhere we have the phenomenon that each folk- or cult-community holds *its* way to be the correct way, and fosters only its rites with painstaking conscientiousness. This is an immediate function of the belief that errors and oversights will have dire consequences, and that in order to be effective, everything must be strictly fulfilled according to the ways of the forefathers as the only "correct way." These compose the very content of the special customs, the folk-customs, the systems of usage as they are practiced in the particular area.

But they are also the specific manner in which special deities and relics are venerated. This veneration is then taught and transmitted as a special priestly art. The common elements of prayer and sacrifice, however, are in all rites. Prayer is based on the idea that the ancestors or gods are powerful, and also merciful and benevolent, if men live according to their will.

In this sense, thanksgiving and praise also belong to prayer. Sacrifice is determined by the idea that ancestors or gods have needs and must subsist on the gifts that are offered to them, or at least be reconciled and pleased through such donations, as a strict lord and patriarch gladly receives even small and worthless gifts as a token of compliant attitude.

The fact that in both prayer and sacrifice the gods are always created in the image of men, and actually according to the image of men's lords and kings, is so obvious that this simple insight could be obscured and reversed only by naive faith in their actual existence—from which authority among men is supposed to be derived.

Likewise, unprejudiced observation cannot but disclose that the deceased and more or less canonized and deified men represent the intermediate stage and connecting link between human and divine rulers, and that the cult of the dead is a transition from veneration which is rendered to chiefs and princes to worship of those divinities who are imagined as the kings of kings.

The concept of *celebration* is commonly related to the ideas of cult and veneration. Festivities bring together those who became separated and who live apart, and they feel themselves reunited in the exaltation of the ceremonies. Quarrels cease and community comes into its own. Thus the festival recalls belongingness and gives it renewed validity. The convening of the clan has something festive about it as does the contemporary family reunion. Fellow-clansmen and countrymen, and finally the believers as such, feel united through common usage and common duty in honoring the ancestor, god or saint. The same thing is true of fellow-workers and other friends. Just as festivals are to this day celebrated to honor men, so, at all times, festivals were celebrated to honor the gods. And custom fixes certain days as holidays.

But if we have become accustomed to associate holidays with joy and jubilation, the gravity and solemnity with which one is supposed to approach the gods stands in certain contrast to that. If we associate the word "holiday" with good cheer, we associate the word "celebration" with solemnity and dignity. In this regard, sacerdotal bearing always remains related to the demeanour of the grieving and mourning, just as the mourning and bewailing of a deceased god or demi-god plays no small role in the most significant religions. To this is added the grief concerning one's own shortcomings and deficiencies, sins and guilts, of which one is ever-conscious in the presence of the much-demanding, jealous gods.

The fact that religious hymns have a grave, heavy rhythm as exemplified by the spondee of Greek verse (significantly so named from offerings to the dead) might be explained by the origin of divine service from the human cult of the dead. Hence the solemn pace of the chorus:

> *Der, streng und ernst, nach alter Sitte,*
> *Mit langsam abgemessnem Schritte*
> *Hervortritt aus dem Hintergrund,*
> *Umwandelnd des Theaters Rund.*

> And staid and solemn, as of old,
> Circling the theatre's wide round,
> With footsteps measured and controlled,
> They vanish in the far background.*

* "The Cranes of Ibycus," *Poetical Works of Friedrich Schiller,* Vol. XVIII of the Weimar Edition; E. P. Arnold-Forster, translator, p. 54.

because the theatre too was an act of cult. Gravity and dignity mark old customs as they should mark old age generally.

* * *

Hence the relationship between custom and religion is of immeasurable significance in the development of culture. The observance of rules which are prescribed by custom for divine service becomes a most sacred and painstaking duty. This is because there is always the idea and the fear that an offense will annoy the deity and bring about the greatest harm to the transgressor and his descendants. If punishments with which the immortals threaten man during his lifetime are frightful, more terrible still are the imaginary phantoms which stare out of eternity at the believer.

The primary unity of the moral code rests in these ideas, as the traditions present us in the Indian *dharma,* the Greek *Themis* and the Roman *fas.* What is at the same time demanded and forbidden through custom and religion, through religion as part of custom and through custom as part of religion, is sacrosanct. Religious custom becomes the most tenacious, the most enduring, precisely because the sanctity of tradition finds support in the sanctity of the object with which it is concerned.

Thus, one might say, it penetrates and nourishes the public and private life of peoples at all stages of culture yet known. The supposition for this is that religion itself contains the faith as inherited and transmitted by our ancestors, the faith of our fathers, that religion thus is a part of custom. W. H. Riehl correctly observes that with the genuine German peasant, custom even now maintains its superiority in this way. ("Even religion is with him not dogma, but custom.")

But what of the establishment of an alien creed and, as it so often happens, its dissemination through the conquerors' fire and sword, if such creed is opposed to custom and native familiar forms of worship which are regarded as an intrinsic part of everything thought to be sacred and necessary? This is an event of formidable hardship for the life and soul of a people. "Burn what you have worshipped, and adore what you have burned" is the password. The new faith takes root, and often what was beloved and good is torn out like an evil weed. The old creed is decried as superstition and heresy, the old gods become mere pseudo-gods, second-class gods, or—as probably happens most frequently— wicked spirits, demons, and devils.

As a rule, it is a new and higher culture which,

with religion and in its forms, penetrates a peasant culture against the wilder life of nomadism, or an urban technique against the crudeness and primitivism of a non-commercial hunting and digging culture. Great improvements and innovations, such as drainage and irrigation systems, bridge-building and techtonic arts have often served as the material bases for new divine as well as human authorities.

These processes of transition are greatly facilitated if they are accompanied by developments which have already taken place within the people and are favored at least by their leaders. The battle, then, against old customs and old beliefs takes place in the name of a nobler "custom" which is established and supported by the new creed. Here the term obviously signifies something other than what is usually essential for custom (the second, instead of the third meaning on page 30).

At any rate, in order to grasp such tremendous changes, we must always remember the influence which, supported by custom and legend, priests and chiefs are able to exercise on both. Indeed their influence is chiefly directed toward preservation, but it also happens from time to time that it is directed toward change, especially if that serves their personal interests. Persuasion, and above all example, can do what the ruler, particularly the alien ruler and conqueror, cannot accomplish by direct force.

A creed is seldom as firm as custom. It can more easily be supplanted if it is preached that it is false, and especially that it is dangerous, that the new gods accomplish greater miracles than the old ones, or that only evil emanates from the old gods, and all good emanates from the new. For adherence to custom and tradition must always dispute and occasionally even fight with the needs, the desires and experiences, and with the opinions derived therefrom about what is good, useful, beneficial and advantageous, or what are the opposite of these.

Through ideas about what is beneficial, ideas about good and evil in a moral sense are affected. And the most efficacious, if not the purest, confirmation for a new moral practice, as for a new doctrine, is that it is assumed to bring forth good fruits— if not in this life, then certainly in a future, in "another" life. And yet custom often maintains its position and proves itself superior even to the most cherished beliefs. The battle between old custom and newer morality, as between old superstition and new dogma, runs through many centuries.

The mania concerning witches and witch-burning,

which lasted in Europe until but a few generations ago, has been a consequence of these struggles. It was imagined that witches and the masters of necromancy had repudiated Christian faith and had dedicated themselves to the service of the devil. Actually the remnants of old pagan cults were surviving which yet were regarded as more authentic and more powerful in realizing certain important purposes:

> *"Eurer Priester summende Gebete*
> *Und ihr Segen haben kein Gewicht"*

> "Murmured chants your priests intone so dourly,
> All their blessings can amend no ill"*

as Goethe's bride of Corinth says.

Probably, all magic—that is, secret magic outlawed and persecuted by publicly acknowledged religious magic—is traceable to such older vanquished but seldom completely destructible forms of divine worship. Sometimes one can discover more than two such overlapping strata of religious ideas and cult forms in which custom is preserved as an extinct animal is preserved in a stone impression.

---

* "The Bride of Corinth," in *Poems of Goethe,* University of North Carolina Studies in the Germanic Languages and Literatures, No. 20, Edwin H. Zeydel, translator (Chapel Hill: University of North Carolina Press, 1957), p. 69.

If custom gives priority to everything which is old, and if this is particularly beneficial to old people, parents, ancestors and forefathers; if the reverence for godheads has been developed chiefly from the ancestor cult itself, then custom and religion together must grant select, prominent social positions and an immense influence to those men who appear to possess through their occupation, and especially through hereditary status, a divine or god-like dignity.

Recognized sorcerers and medicine men—that is, the priesthood—is such a status which can, in this sense, rise far above the people. It is cultivated through the functions of cults, particularly through the correct and artistically perfect execution of sacrifices. Even though the domestic sacrifice can still be completed by every father of a family, particularly if offerings are only given to his own ancestors, the household gods, the sacrifice for the community, for the people, becomes an accomplishment which presumes mysterious knowledge.

Such knowledge can be transmitted only through practice and teaching. Indeed, according to deeply rooted beliefs, the talent and capacity for it can be transmitted only hereditarily. The priesthood, whether or not it is hereditary, is a *paternal* status group. The honorary title of father and patriarch is repeated in many forms. The infallible high-priest of the Roman Church is called "papa," the "abbot" is also derived from a word which means "father" in Syriac, and the word "priest" is derived from the Greek word for the "elder."

The dignity of the elder (men) was transferred from the synagogue to the old Christian community. Indeed, the reformative movement strove to restore Christianity to this priestless origin, whereby the baptismal sects were the most radical—and the Calvinists proceeded at least more consequentially than the Lutherans. Here, the names of Presbyter and Presbyterium are revived, so to speak, in rebelling against their descendants who are personified in the names Priest and Priesthood. Similar occurrences can often be observed.

Priests go far in the audacity of their self-assertion when they fancy themselves equal or similar to the gods. And from there it is only one step to the representation or governorship of God ascribed, for instance, to the "holy father." The occupants of the Chair of Peter have not been at all hesitant to take this step. According to Catholic dogma, every consecrated priest, at the moment when he changes the host into the body of Christ before the altar, becomes invested with divine dignity, just as the sorcerers are always regarded as sons of God.

The Indian priestly caste is inflated with even more arrogance. In Vishnu, the Lawbook, it is written: "The gods are the invisible deities, and the Brahmans the visible ones. The Brahmans maintain the world. Gods dwell in heaven through the grace of the Brahmans." And, it should be added, the Brahmans (as such) live on earth through the popular will of custom.

The spiritual and the secular community—church and state—were originally indivisible. And the spiritual, as the elder component, enjoys not only higher reverence in religion (which is self-evident), but also higher reverence in custom. But secular as well as spiritual dignity and privilege is traceable to the dignity and prerogatives of the elders. This is also true where and insofar as they develop independently of the spiritual ones.

Etymologically, nobility in German (*Adel*) recalls the age (*Alter*) of the family, which, apart from the material basis, is the root of esteem and partly also of political power which, even in modern constitutions, is conceded to the "old and established" landed gentry. Justus Moser who had a particularly well developed sense for everything old in customs and institutions, once remarked that the esteem which one renders noble birth apparently springs from the reverence which is rendered the old.

That esteem is not weakened even though many old people ultimately become childish. Rather, it seems to Moser that one might honor high birth without ever similarly honoring any one person of high birth if there is reason why he does not deserve this esteem. Indeed, the role which the nobility and dynasties heading it have played in public life as of old is in many ways analogous to the role of old men under simple family and community conditions. The Council of the Elders—the *Gerusie* or Senate—was or became as a rule a council of nobility. The old have experience, and wisdom is attributed to age. In any case, it is thought that they know tradition and custom, and thus also law and propriety, insofar as these rest in tradition and custom and are meant to serve as a norm according to general agreement.

The point is well taken that the authority of the old must have been greater in communities which could learn nothing from written documents, and which were thus forced to rely even for facts on oral tradition. But, under any circumstances, the influence of the old is a mighty potential for conservation and stability: they balance the restlessness and novelty-seeking tendencies of youth and sometimes attempt to restore the obsolete.

A similar but not precisely equivalent phenomenon is the clinging of whole status groups, such as nobility and priesthood, to tradition which grants them more or less superhuman authority. There is frequently, though not always, something senile about them. As ruins, they yet survive in this way in the modern civilizations of Europe. So long as both were in their prime, they fought bitterly with one another. The two swords have tended to clash on earth.

But the authority of the old family—including the dynasty which also often rests more in power than in custom—is too precarious an authority if left completely self-reliant. It also demands unction and sanctification, the mystic seal. It claims divine grace and divine right as an immediate privilege of the crown, just as the bishops, in spite of the popes, have claimed this up to the most recent times. In truth, spiritual and secular authority are one in origin, both being sanctified by custom. They spring from the womb of superstition which is impregnated ever anew by the spirit of the people.

Derivation from the authority of the patriarch and the domestic priest is still definitely noticeable in both. The king, as commander-in-chief, *needs* the grace and assistance of the gods. As a judge, he needs enlightenment and inspiration in order to find truth and justice. Often enough, his esteem is a function of the belief that he may be a descendant of the gods, or even that he himself may be a god.

Christians resolutely refused to worship the genius of the Roman emperor. For that reason they were branded wicked citizens and were hated and despised (as always heretics and dissidents, religious *or* political, are hated and despised because they do not worship the prevailing idols, and because they prefer to *think* rather than to merely reiterate).

Everywhere we find spiritual and secular governmental functions partly mixed, partly—in spite of their rivalry and jealousy—working beside and with each other. Both do not always work in the sense of conservation, of custom, of tradition. It is precisely their antagonism to one another, combined with the thorn of economic necessity, which often puts the one as well as the other power in the direction of change, innovation, or progress. But each of them will always be anxious to cover the new with the garment of the old and, whenever

possible, to characterize an innovation as mere re-
vival of a former practice.

Old and new needs meet, especially in the great
sphere of public and private law. I can only intimate
here how powerfully efficacious custom, as well as
religion, is in this respect. The words "customary
law" and "customs of law" point to this fact. What
is reverentially called the "unwritten law," in antiquity, constitutes law as it exists and is established
by custom.

But at the same time it is in its widest sense
natural law, according to the original meaning of
this concept. Indeed, the natural must also be the
ancient, which goes back into time immemorial and
which is the Holy of Holies for custom. What has
always been is accepted as self-evident by contemporary custom.

In this sense the Hindu developed the doctrine
of *rita* as the legal concept which we (according
to Leist) may take as the common idea of Aryans
before their separation. In this idea, as it is developed in the *Veda,* the regulation of nature is iden-
tified as one with the regulation of human life.
Sunlight and moonlight, the alternation of day and
night, dawn announcing the appearance of the sun,
and the two charioteers of the "Cloud Stallions"—

this unaltering, imperturbably fixed order of the heavens, the eternal regulation of time, is combined in the *Veda* with the actual physical order of the earth, and as such they coincide. The existence of fertilizing rivers, the nurture-giving cow, the dualism of sexes among gods, men and animals; the institution of marriage, of clans, of domestic and royal power; the settling of men in their homestead; protected possession; the phenomenon of illness, regarded partly as natural, partly as an expression of divine punishment; the responsibility of man for his evil deeds—all this is the eternal, unalterable order of *Varuna* or *Mithra,* and this order is *rita.*

The Latin *ratum* means the established, the fixed; hence *ratio* means the established, objectively-real natural order as well as reason bound to it and discerning it. In a similar sense, although confined to living beings, a later Roman jurist defines natural law as the "law" that nature has taught all animals, and cites as examples the separation by sex, the rearing of children, etc. The custom of man is here completely bound will which can only confirm and develop what is also the custom of animals as their manner of doing things.

But at that time a wholly different concept of natural law had already evolved, which sets the reasonable (because purposeful) arrangement of things in *contrast* to custom and tradition. The *separation* of law from custom is linked to similar ideas. Even customary law is in principle comprehended as something different from and distinct from custom. In the first place, custom always wills that something come to pass. The legal order, including customary law, intends that a rule be valid, and that in particular the judge, while judging, be bound by it. Law is *pronounced* and custom is *followed*. Custom can thus more easily be called an unwritten law than an unwritten right.

Hirzel has correctly noted and stressed that law does not always stem from custom, but that custom occasionally evolves from law based on reason. ("Philologisch-historische klasse," *Abhandlungen,* [Leipzig: Königliche Sächsische Gesellshaft der Wissenschaften, 1900], Vol. 20, No. 1, pp. 1-98.) Christian theocracy again adopted natural law in its original sense by equating *jus naturale* with *jus divinum.*

❉ ❉ ❉

I have deduced that custom characteristically endows a privilege on age and hence that it desires authority and government by the old, from which government by high clergy and secular aristocracy develops. The connection between custom and religion and of either one with law was therewith explained.

But custom has yet another preference. For clarification of this, I draw attention to the fact that custom was originally of the male gender in Germanic. That is to say, custom has a pronounced partiality for women. And this partiality is requited. It is just as reciprocal as that between custom and the old. Is this relationship also derivable from the pattern of custom and tradition? I maintain an affirmative answer to this question.

The general distinction which we make between the old and the young is that the old *preceded* the new and the young, that the young originate and are descendants of the old. The consciousness of descent is more immediately related to the mother than the father; it is stronger and more sensual. Together with the greater burden, the mother obtains the greater honor. We count our lives from the womb and we absorb our ancestors' sentiments with maternal milk.

If the Israelites, who were definitely a *patriarchal* people, had the male created as the original human being—Adam means Man—and had the woman be a product of his rib, then it follows that their law commands "Honor thy father and thy mother." According to the sentiment and the ways of thinking of more ancient times and earlier peoples, the command would have been "Honor thy mother and thy father."

In the second half of the nineteenth century, a noteworthy and significant discovery threw new light on the antiquity of the human race. Bachofen, the Basel scholar of jurisprudence, must be recognized as the originator. This discovery was "matriarchy," the discovery that patriarchal institutions (which were so prevalent among historical peoples) were preceded in many (and, one could suppose, in *all*) cases, by matriarchal ones. The latter are found even today among some Indian tribes, and even more among the Australian Negroes, although often already in dissolution in transition to the seigneurial rights of males.

To say that among peoples who have been arrested at a primitive stage of culture the rule of males is often a distinctive feature, while apparently matriarchy arises only with the progressing peoples, when the son-in-law is received into the household of the father-in-law (as Jacob in that of Laban) is certainly no argument against the greater immediacy of maternal authority.

Bachofen relates his learned study to a phrase

of Herodotus about the Lycaeans, wherein it is said that the latter have a custom which deviates from all other peoples'. That is, they are named according to the mother rather than according to the father. If one should ask anyone about his origin, he would enumerate his maternal ancestors. Also, the question of whether or not the child is considered legitimate would be settled through the mother. The marriage of a native woman with a slave would be valid in this case, but not that of a native male with an alien wife.

Bachofen tries to prove that Greek mythology is filled with the traces and remnants of concepts rooted in such ruling positions of women and the higher rank of the mother. His explanation of the legend of Orestes has become famous. The Erynian Furies, as goddesses of revenge, that terrible tribe of the night, belong to the sinister deities of the depths, of which Faust's journey through hell to the "mothers" is reminiscent.

The cult of Mother Earth and its spirits belongs to matriarchy. The generations of the living have sprung from the dark womb of the earth in much the same way as light issues from the bosom of the night. The "great mother," Mother Nature, works everywhere in mysterious obscurity.

The worship of deities residing in heaven is linked with the concept of fatherhood. Zeus, the father of god and men, and his son of light Apollo, his valiant daughter Athena, are carriers of the new principle which was destined to become a ruling principle. The Furies pursue the mother's murderer, Apollo fights them, and Athena, the motherless Walkyrie, provides him with forgiveness. She establishes the court of justice which is to try the mother murderer. As the adherents of the old and the new laws are balanced, she makes the decision in his favor (through *calculus Minervae* which indeed is subject to different interpretations). In Aeschylus' tragedy, she expressly gives as her reason that no mother has borne her:

> For me no mother bore within her womb,
> And, save for wedlock evermore eschewed,
> I vouch myself the champion of the man,
> Not of the woman, yea, with all my soul,—
> In heart, as birth, a father's child alone.
> Thus will I not too heinously regard
> A woman's death who did her husband slay,
> The guardian of her home. . . .*

This means that the mother as such is no longer

* From Aeschylus' *The Eumenides; The Complete Greek Drama,* Vol. 1, edited by Whitney J. Oates and Eugene O'Neill, Jr. (New York: Random House, Inc., 1938), p. 297.

sacred to her! And in a bitter, repeated lament to
the dark night, her mother, the spirits of revenge
cry:

> Woe on you, younger gods! the ancient right
> Ye have o'erridden, rent it from my hands.†

But the women maintain their realm in custom
as well as in the natural order:

"Mächtig seid ihr, ihr seid's durch der Gegenwart ruhigen
*   Zauber.*
Was die stille nicht wirkt, wirket die rauschende nie.
Kraft erwart' ich vom Mann, des Gesetzes Würde
*   behaupt' er,*
Aber durch Anmut allein herrschet und herrsche das
*   Weib."*

Mighty thou art in the strength of thy calm unruffled
    enchantments;
For tranquility's spell bustle can never achieve.
Force I expect in man, defending the canons of order;
But let woman alone through her amenity rule.‡

This is Schiller's contemplation. But to him we
also owe the poem, "Honor to Women."

---

† From Aeschylus' *The Eumenides; The Complete Greek Drama*,
Vol. 1, edited by Whitney J. Oates and Eugene O'Neill, Jr. (New
York: Random House, Inc., 1938), p. 298.

‡ "The Influence of Woman," *Poetical Works of Friedrich Schiller*, Vol. XVIII of the Weimar Edition; E. P. Arnold-Forster,
translator, p. 256.

> *"In der Mutter bescheidener Hütte*
> *Sind sie geblieben mit schamhafter Sitte,*
> *Treue Töchter der frommen Natur,"*

> "True Daughter of Nature, she loves not to roam,
> But meekly with Nature forever at home,
> By the Mother, still dwelleth the child"*

he says of the women, who recall, with seductive
and captivating glances, the young men longing
for the distant. And, in the final verse,

> *"Aber mit sanft überredender Bitte*
> *Führen die Frauen das Szepter der Sitte,*
> *Löschen die Zwietracht, die tobend entglüht.*
> *Lehren die Kräfte, die feindlich sich hassen,*
> *Sich in der lieblichen Form zu umfassen,*
> *Und vereinen, was ewig sich flieht."*

But woman her throne by persuasion defends.
O'er the realm of the Manners her scepter extends
  Our strength she subdues to her will.
All forces at war with each other she charms,
The discord she quenches, the hate she disarms;
  Ever-binding—what flies from her still!†

"Honor women" the poem begins. And this is
exactly what is intended by custom, in contrast to
the brutality and coarseness of men, who caress the

---

* "Honor to Women," *The Poems and Ballads of Schiller,* Sir
Edward Bulwer Lytton, Bart., translator (New York: Thomas Y.
Crowell and Co.), p. 197.
  † *Ibid.,* pp. 198-99.

weaker sex today while abusing it tomorrow. And this honor should be rendered to women as such, and thus also to maidens. But the symbol of reverence for women is not so much the maiden, who seeks to attract and captivate through her charm, as it is the maternal woman, the matron. She has presentiments and prophetic wisdom, knows healing herbs and magic formulas. Thus we detect her in religion and in superstition—as the prophetess, Erda, from Nordic mythology appears in Wagner's *Nibelungenring,* and Pythia murmurs her dark words of oracles, enraptured by the steams rising from the soil.

The Norns of our sagas, the Sibyls in the Romans', who had foretold the advent of Christianity—in these and many another form folk poetry expresses accumulated experiences about the specific talents of many a woman who had become serene through life's struggle, just as Tacitus states that the Germans venerated in women something visionary and sacred. This was not specific of the Teutons although it may particularly fit their temperament.

Even among other ancient peoples there was a counterpoise in custom and in religion against the power of males, confirmed by law because they enacted the law. Everywhere we find woman participating in distinguished places in cult as well as in magic. Her soul is directed more intensely toward the religious than is the mind of man. The prudent awe of piety corresponds more to the nature of women than the pride of trust in one's own strength, of conquering knowledge and weighing criticism. Superstition and belief in miracles are more natural to the imagination of a woman than doubt and inquiry, and more congenial to it than clear and stark cognition.

Hence the liaison between women and religion, just as that between women and custom, is a relationship of mutual affirmation. Custom demands awe; at least it demands respect. It gives the woman her unique rank and requires that males are considerate toward the "fragile, vulnerable sex," especially its "pregnant" circumstances, its "good hope," which under sound conditions is also the father's hope; and it demands that loyal kin and neighbors participate in it.

Often custom works much the more in favor of the woman the less rights are granted her. In England, up to 100 years ago, the woman was almost completely without rights and even so, England was regarded as the "paradise of women." Perhaps custom is precisely in such an anomaly reminiscent of older, if not more primitive, times, for custom has as a rule become everything which is opposed to the rule of might. We are still replete with customs which are brutal. But custom, according to its predominant direction, has a humane character.

Custom—or is it morals or morality? Much has been both thought and written about the relation between custom and morality. R. von Jhering, in particular, attempts to portray, in his very penetrating researches, both the common and distinct features of custom and morality in, as it were, anatomical preparations. According to him, "language" —that is, the German language—points out the contrast between the exterior and the interior, the form and the substance of behaviors, and custom refers only to the form, the manner, the conduct. Morality refers to the substance, the value, the character.

In his more detailed discussion, Jhering states that morals forbid that which is evil *per se*, whereas custom forbids merely the dangerous, lest evil result from it. Custom may be termed the security police of morality; it may be localized, restricted to one "class"—that is, the upper stratum of society. Thus custom may be exclusive, because it only takes root in fertile (favorable) soil. Jhering always thinks of custom (and I shall revert to this later) only as rules of behavior, but this contradicts the usage of language which he chooses to be his guide.

We differentiate custom and morality not according to their objects, but according to the viewpoints under which they are considered. A distinction can be expressed in one short sentence: "Custom is fact, and morality is idea." Hence custom is thought of as a property of a people or of a country, and morality is conceived of as something universally human. Custom *is,* but morality *demands.* We also say "custom prescribes," but the meaning of this statement implies that as a rule it is actually done. This meaning is indeed the prevailing meaning, and custom as *will* had to be derived from it.

Morals, on the contrary, are thought of as something *demanding,* or which issue stronger or more lax prescripts and prohibitions which, however, are all too often not obeyed. They maintain their validity even though they may not be perceived and accepted. I compare the distinction between custom and morality with that between money and credit, and this illustrates what they have in common. Money, when paid, contains a demand. This may be a demand that commodities be given or that receipts be rendered. An obligation, however, is in essence a demand, and morality is often a bill of exchange which is not honored.

And yet money and credit are so closely related that there are quite a few intermediate stages between them. A good bill of exchange is like cash, and our bank-notes circulate as money even if they are nothing but claims on a bank. Similarly, custom and morality are not only namesakes, but legitimate cousins. Indeed, they are occasionally related to one another like siblings. This is where women enter in, and—as in life—found the relationship of affinity and make the connection. Morality is to a great extent, and in a significant way, chiefly the will and the interest of women. As such, morality has permeated custom.

Inversely, the conservation and care of custom *in regard to* women has become, *through* women, part of morality as it is at least theoretically recognized, and often has become religiously sanctioned. As such it has, as good and refined custom, been detached from base customs and from bad habits. But also it is known by another title which points up its ideal character: demeanor, good breeding, propriety—in a word, *decorum*. That which *should be* is always derived most easily from that which *has always been,* hence also from that which is exemplary, deserving of imitation. Duty derives from that which is usually done. For it appears self-evident that one must do that which everyone does, which "one" does, and hence what the "best," the "esteemed," the "good" society does; what is regarded as "refined." And if this latter always or even only chiefly were "good" in the moral sense, more of it would be found than is the case.

But this has come to pass in some measure in the exterior forms of *savoir vivre,* which were formerly accurately termed "minor morality," or the teachings of it as the complement of ethics (*Ethica complementaria,* hence "compliments"). The notion that certain ways of acting are not fitting to, and indeed are disfiguring to the actor, reflects on vanity and thus on a strong incentive. This notion thus becomes a screen and a shield for women against the "audacity" of men. Hence Goethe has the Princess in Tasso say:

> "Wo Sittlichkeit regiert, regieren sie,
> Und wo die Frechheit herrscht, da sind sie nichts,
> Und wirst du die Geschlechter beide fragen:
> Nach Freiheit strebt der Mann, das Weib nach Sitte."

Propriety surrounds as with a wall
Their tenderness and frailty. Where it rules,

They rule; where insolence is lord, then they
Are nothing. Ask both sexes, you will find
Man strives for freedom, woman strives for rules."*

which is definitely thought of in the sense of old custom and transmitted forms of life. For today the struggle for freedom would undoubtedly be ascribed to a great part of the female world, at least to the younger ones, and perhaps even more than to men —at least more than to men of higher social positions.

The fact that, aside from its general meaning, the word "morality" has acquired the particular meaning of *sexual* morality, is clearly related to the relation of the feminine spirit to custom. For sexual morality has, according to its nature, an intimate relationship with shame. The observance of shame (in some manner, for although it exists in very different forms, it exists wherever there is civilization) is both demanded and effected through custom in the mutual relations of the sexes.

Despite many aberrations and peculiarities, it can be recognized as a common, ancient inheritance of the human race that custom limits freedom of the relationship between the sexes in that its purpose

* Johann Wolfgang von Goethe, *Torquato Tasso,* translated by Ben Kimpel and T. C. Duncan Eaves (Fayetteville: University of Arkansas, 1956), p. 27.

is to check savagery and disorder. Everywhere, the rules made for men differ from those made for women, and those made for the old differ from the young's. Partially intended to set limits between the sexes generally, and partially for the unmarried specifically, who are drawn together by instinct and affection, these rules establish boundaries, give moderation, and allow reason rather than passion to rule.

Here as elsewhere, custom—aside from the fact that it is rooted in tradition—is the will of the elders, particularly of the parents, who regard it as their duty and to their own advantage to guard their children and protect them from imprudence. Where custom is strict, it demands not only "virtuous"— that is, discreet, modest behavior, which is particularly demanded of young maidens—but chastity as well, unless marriage or at least betrothal gives the man a right to the woman.

As is well known, custom condemns adulterous or prenuptial fornication of the woman more vigorously than that of the man. Custom is particularly jealous in guarding the chastity and fidelity of the woman. What is the basis for this? Chiefly the mentality and will of women themselves, since they regard their purity as a valuable possession, which the virgin should only surrender to her husband whom she loves or respects as her master. If she values that treasure highly enough, she will surrender it only in return for enduring protection granted to her and to the children. Because women look upon marriage as the most precious thing in their life, and because marriage is the common interest of women, chastity is the honor of their status. And a frivolous woman or one who sells herself loses caste, branded not only as a fool but as a traitoress.

Feminine solidarity in matters of their own sex becomes a special subject of custom. This solidarity is all the more successful since women play an active role in the maintenance and cultivation of custom. The will of the men meets them halfway, not only insofar as they, too, do something for custom's sake, but also—and chiefly—because the value of woman as a good is enhanced through virginity and, in marriage, through fidelity. But men by themselves do not easily develop a reciprocal custom. Chastity has no such immediate value for them for the simple reason that among men, as among other mammals and vertebrates, the female is the wooed and desired sex, much as this natural relationship may be obscured by cultural institutions.

But so far as the female knows herself to be wooed, she has every reason to be sparing with her favors, especially if she is one of those who are desired for other reasons than their personal charm—for instance, their fathers' cows (dowry). Even if the maiden makes her own choice, she is *still* the giving one, and man is still the receiver. Even if man makes himself attractive and pleasing, and parades his strength in order to attract the woman, there is not anything analogous to female solidarity with regard to the condition of his body. Other males have no instinctual interest in whether or not the groom is chaste, because the marriage of individual men is a matter of indifference to them so far as sex is concerned. For woman *as* woman, on the other hand, marriage, and thus her value *for* marriage, is her most significant concern.

Modesty, which is more natural to woman than to man because it is rooted in fear and in shyness, is manifested in its most primitive form as concealment. The urge to cover certain parts of the body, and chiefly the genitals, is indeed (as the observation of our children as well as ethnology indicates) hardly an innate instinct. However, it may be manifested in a certain rather early stage of development, and it remains independent of other purposes which clothing serves, as it is sometimes replaced by tattooing and painting the skin.

Custom here, as is so often the case, fixes and orders what was otherwise wavering and arbitrary. It establishes certain "costumes," above all the special costume of women in distinction to that of men. To these, further distinctions are fixed, such as unmarried women from the married and the widows, the youth from the man, and the master from the servant. Clothing becomes a *symbol* of sex as well as of marital status, office, or prestige. Hence the great significance of investiture in custom and in religion. Manners other than covering or emphasizing or adorning parts of the body, like the objects of ornament and utility, also belong to "costume."

For custom, everything becomes significant as a sign or as a symbol, and in this it is reinforced by religion. Custom and religion intend to differentiate and distinguish by perceptible characteristics; they intend that everyone observe and respect what the symbols impress on his eye, his ear and his memory. In these matters, both custom and religion are everywhere, and particularly, for the peoples of early stages of culture, the natural, convenient, revered and sanctified lawgivers. So profound has the union of custom and costume become that, as is well known, "costume" has its name from habit.

A certain measure of freedom remains within custom. Here the desire of the woman to please, to attract, or to charm often meets and conflicts with the sense of modesty which is ingrained in her and sanctioned by custom. The lust of woman for ornament and finery, and her aesthetic sense which is so profoundly related to her moral sense, are nourished by her desire to please. Indeed, because of this, they are often at odds with one another. The former demands the beautiful and the brilliant, and the latter demands respectability or "propriety." In the former, freedom is exercised, and in the latter obedience to custom.

And if I have termed the cult of the dead the custom of customs, then its high significance is also proven by the fact that it silences or subdues the desire for adornment. The sense of beauty desires the complete and the pure, the resplendent and the light, and the differentiation of color. It desires to express and to inspire joy. But custom demands dark or plain white garments as signs of mourning. Custom even demands that one should tear one's clothes and cover one's head with sack-

cloth and ashes. Custom wishes to give style to
the expression of sentiment: dirt and destruction
seem to be appropriate for grief, since grief is partially related to anger and vexation, and partially
it has "no time" to guide attention and care into
the usual directions.

❈   ❈   ❈

If custom as social will refers to the life and welfare of a community, then reproduction must be
of particularly high significance. If its glance is
directed toward the past and old age, here it is
directed toward youth and into the future. Wooing
and mating are ever new and yet the oldest tradition; and the woman, in giving life and nurture,
is bound to nature and hence to custom (which very
largely only makes the natural into law). However,
quite often custom departs from nature and prescribes the unnatural, indeed things contrary to
nature, under the influence of superstitious ideas.

On the other hand, it often changes the natural
in that it wishes to ennoble it. The woman's childbed is not commanded, but suggested and recom-
mended by nature. Custom gives it its form and its
limits: the house is decorated, wicked spells are
warded off and the beneficial spirits are brought
forth. The woman in childbed receives the visits

of neighbors, she is subjected to ceremonial baths (which are frequently unclean), and finally she is blessed or brought to a church; this involves elaborate feasts, such as christening feasts.

Thus far everything follows. But there is no natural reason for the ancient custom of the couvade (the father's childbed) which still exists in Europe among the Basques and is a genuine and obligatory, if astounding custom. This is explicable only on the basis of faith in the mysterious relationship between begetter and begotten, which necessitates the cautious handling of wicked spirits, and therefore fasting and chastisement.

Custom makes better sense when it ascribes to the father and the mother their respective tasks in rearing the child, and when it establishes the obligations of nursing and tender care and, on the other hand, discipline and strictness toward the offspring. To be sure, the barbaric practices of exposure and sale of children, even of infanticide, especially of girls, survive even among peoples of higher civilizations. Nevertheless, the force of custom to protect the helpless child as a valuable possession prevails until it appears as the absolute and the only natural practice.

But because procreation is so important, cohabitation of man and wife—marriage—is sacred. The community must participate in it by endorsing the marriage which it chooses to or is obliged to recognize. Custom requires festive participation. The wedding couple, like the bride's parents and kinfolk, must perform certain procedures which are appropriate to the validation or at least to the correct blessing of the nuptials; incantations and religious rituals should not be absent. In wedding customs there is a suggestion of primitive procedures of establishing marriage, which are reminiscent of a more barbaric, but also gayer way of life. These earlier usages are comparable to the rudimentary organs of animals and of men in that they no longer have real functions. They are survivals which are preserved although they are no longer understood. For what is implied—that is, their significance and their purpose—constitutes the real life of usages and of custom.

However, it also happens than when the old meaning has been forgotten, a newer one is given to a usage; thus an atrophied practice gains new vigor. In this way, too, tissues and organs gain new life, in that they are modified to adjust to new circumstances of life. And perhaps the real meaning of many a usage is reduced to an unreal one, and finally to a mere sign for existing situations, to a symbol, just as the meanings of words. And often a considerable part of usage consists in the pronouncing of words or sentences and sometimes in significant actions. In some royal houses, one can still find the practice of the bride's distributing pieces of her garter to the male guests before departure. This practice, which is now but a sign of graciousness, is rooted in the concept that the whole clan had a right to the defloration of the virgin—a right which might have been exercised by a chief or a priest, but at least must have been redeemed at a valid wedding.

Similarly, many an old peasant custom is traceable to obscure ideas about the marriageable girl being the common possession of men. Hence the "bundling," the nocturnal visits through which the unbetrothed, unmarried girl makes preliminary acquaintance with youths. To be sure, custom sets limits to this intimacy, and the idea prevails that while every young man is the potential spouse, the actual taking possession—the *consummatio* of canon law—after betrothal (consensus) makes the favored lover the *actual* spouse. Custom prescribes and seals the natural basis of the ceremonial act—the transition to his hand, and also possibly to his sib. The religious ceremony is essentially an *accompaniment to* the establishment of this union, and not essential to it.

It is the religion of the family which is at the basis of all cult. The ancestors' spirits, which hover about the domestic hearth, are supposed to participate in such a solemn celebration, and are supposed to approve of the bride's forsaking her home. The new altar, which she should guard and honor from that day forward, must receive her kindly. This was the custom of the Greeks whose sense of beauty permeates their way of life as well as their art.

In this instance religion is completely absorbed into custom. The priest, who among more primitive peoples has to perform magic ritual, is not necessarily a participant. Nor was he in Christianity until the time when his authority was already endangered and in decline. Further, since law had excluded him through the establishment of the civil marriage, custom retains him and demands the religious "consecration" of the union.

Here, as elsewhere, *religious* custom is most permanent as the custom of *domestic* life, family custom, which as such is also folk custom. The home is the abode of the most intimate and warmest living together, and the abode of habit. But custom has relatively little free play here because the family is ordinarily ruled in a patriarchal fashion. In broad culture areas, such as the Chinese, it is still today the large, undivided family in which the married sons and even grandsons remain with their wives and children. Nevertheless the family is also "folk" —and this is all the more true the larger it is.

The cooperative element which exists beside the patriarchal one is sometimes, as in the Southern Slavic house community, even the predominant element. Here the community elects its chief and can depose him. But even when chieftainship is hereditary in the clans, it is based on the custom of the house community. For the "law of succession" actually rests in custom. Indeed, in our individual families, the cultivation of particular customs has little free play, but common custom penetrates it. Neither the parents themselves nor their children nor servants can evade custom. Many a common celebration is retained by custom after its religious meaning has become weakened (like the modern Christmas) or is even adopted by those outside of the religion to which it is related (as the selfsame holiday celebrated by contemporary Jews).

So every family also has its special holidays, particularly birthdays, the essence of which is that they designate the annual return of the day of birth. The birthday gives expression to human equality and fraternity, since even the lowliest has a birthday and the first birthday of an infant already has meaning for parents and siblings.

On the other hand, it is the custom of a birthday celebration which shows that persons have more or less significance and importance in the home and in wider circles, so that the birthday of the prince becomes a legal holiday. A widespread custom, which is especially observed in more recent times, demands that the birthdays of highly esteemed men and women be celebrated, especially if they reach a rounded-off age in higher figures (as sixty, seventy, and so forth).

The custom of gift-giving is particularly relevant to the birthday. And the ancient custom of expressing, through presents, homage or admiration of the powerful, whose status approaches that of the gods, is preserved in a changed form. Even the offering is a voluntary tribute of commoners and of subjects. In this sense the gift is an expression of humility and of devotion which, so to speak, does not claim anything of its own but which allows everything he might desire to belong to the master. The giver is grateful enough if the modest gift is accepted kindly.

Always the gift means a type of communism which is more freely expressed among equals. According to a Hellenic saying, the goods of friends are communal goods. Thus the custom of establishing marriage simply through giving gifts to the bride's parents signifies a condition wherein ownership is almost non-existent. And little distinction is made in terms of property. The practice of wife-purchase necessarily developed from this. This custom often makes it impossible for the poor to obtain a wife unless she is won through service or through rape. Under primitive conditions, younger sons are often compelled to resort to this. Wedding gifts are probably also founded upon an old clan- and village-type communism in which custom, by demanding such gifts, allows the young couple and their household to obtain what is due them.

A lighter duty, which is widely applicable, is that of sharing joy and sorrow, of congratulating and of making condolences. In this case, subordinates and minors have special cause to be circumspect in order to preserve or to obtain the good will of those in power. However, custom always functions as a balancing force and a reciprocity, since it requires that gratitude and sometimes reciprocation be given. This is because it is based on community and friendship. It is essentially the habit which strengthens what otherwise originates in casual sentiments of appreciation, love and reverence. This is the case however deeply interest and scheming may be intermingled with, or become the dominant motive in the sentiments of lowlier ones.

But all common dependency functions as an equalizer, particularly in the case of the ancestors and the gods. The higher these are placed, the more does the distance between mortals disappear. Participation in domestic cult even elevated the slave who, when introduced into the house of the Greek, was sprinkled with holy water and fed at the holy hearth. Even among the Romans he was protected by the household gods and his grave was sacred.

The notions that the weak, the miserable, the beggar, the fugitive, and even the pursued criminal receive divine protection, and that it is an outrage to dishonor the stranger, are rooted in natural pity. Pity is particularly aroused in women through pathetic appearance, through tears, and pleas. These sentiments may be combined with curiosity, the wish to barter and to sell, if the stranger carries unusual goods with him, or if he is even a trader.

And the esteem of the person most likely would never fail to influence the way in which the guest is received.

It can be assumed that humanity obtains a powerful support through the idea that the gods are particularly benevolent toward the miserable. And it was no accident that the Greeks and Romans made the highest god the guardian of hospitality. It was supposed that even the stranger would honor him, and that before him even the rich and the powerful are small. According to Greek and Roman custom, hospitality, which was understood to be reciprocal, was established by offering the right hand, by the guest's gift, and especially by the common meal.

Even today the festive board has a similar dignity; the banquet is intended to bring about peace and happiness. The Romans called it simply *convivium,* while the Greek term *symposion* points up the peculiar meaning which was attributed as of old to drinking together, the lusty drinking "bouts."

The creed which is symbolized in the drinking of blood is particularly effective here, since blood *unites,* and because every original unity stems from this specific liquid. Hence a hundred years ago and even later, among German youths, the custom of blood brotherhood was not only nominal; drops of one's own blood were mingled with others' in a beaker which was emptied with linked arms. Drinking from the same beaker continues to be a symbol of friendship, and the offering of a beaker from which one has first sipped is a symbol of hospitality.

After the usage of vessels had become more individualized, reminiscences of this usage became evident in the drinking of toasts, in the touching together of glasses which, as it were, desire to become one. The German word *schenken* originally stems from the drink that is poured and proffered. In extending the meaning of this word to all vestiges of gift-giving, the universality and the meaningfulness of this custom are perceptible.

Wundt was undoubtedly correct in tracing the *pourboire* to this custom of hospitality. But he apparently did not see that the meaning of this word connotes more than a form of voluntary *wages*. It is also generalized in every voluntary but intentional and calculated donation. Hence the "tip" includes also the bribe. Wundt may also be questioned in his statement that the tip may be a noteworthy example of a custom, the original meaning of which has been completely changed into its contrary. From a symbol of friendship it became an expression of the servant-master relationship. It is not the acceptance of gifts, but of monetary donations, which characterizes the servant. The wealthy, the men of rank, the lords are characterized precisely by the fact that they have money in abundance. But they gladly accept as presents what the lowly can give because *they* produce it: the fruits of their labor.

Even the wage is originally thought of as a monetary present, given to boot, while lodgings and board —possibly also clothing (their "livery")—should counterbalance the service rendered. Naturally such supplement also may be promised and, in hiring and recruiting, an "advance" or *handsel* is given. Even today, domestic servants get a part of their remuneration in Christmas gifts which, although dependent upon custom, may yet be assured, hence promised, to them.

The personal rendering of service always has something of the tribute, and thus of the gift element, in it. This is manifested in the fact that under many circumstances men aspire to service as to an honor—service at court is an example of this. Naturally hope for reward and other benefits are linked to this aspiration. State and communal service is still essentially thought of as an honorary office;

from that follows compensation, remuneration, *salaire* (salt money), lodging money and, finally, a regular salary; but many purely honorary offices yet remain. Thus what the author and the artist receive is also interpreted as an honorary donation—honorarium—not as a salary or payment, because it is not the equivalent. Now and then they exceed its limits but in the great majority of cases they fall far short of them.

Custom ever signifies community. And because blood is the basis of the most intimate community, drinking together has even more value than eating together. In the Christian sacrament of the Lord's Supper (the Eucharist), partaking of the bread and wine as the body and blood of the Lord is supposed to express spiritual union with Him and at the same time the unity of the communicants among themselves. No wonder that the priesthood retained the prerogative of the chalice which contains His blood, and that the faithful waged passionate, bloody battle for the gratification, the lay chalice, of which they were deprived. Hence it is a token or sign of separation from the Roman Church to receive the holy meal "in either form."

However significant it may be to drink blood, he who imbibes prefers the blood of the vine or of other intoxicating beverages. And the necessity or desire to quench one's thirst is related in manifold forms to custom, with its peaceful-sociable purpose. It is very common for the drinker to toast the "health" of his confreres, or for them to drink together from a drinking-horn or a goblet, or to drink the health of a third by touching their beakers or glasses together.

In fact, custom demands this at times. For example, one drinks the health of engaged couples, the newly wed, the parents and relatives of both kin, the health of a christened infant, the birthday-child, the jubilees as among family celebrations, or that of kings, ministers, or mayors at public feasts. In addition, there is the custom of giving short toasts or long table speeches which are named after the word for browned bread (toast), because the English custom prescribes that speeches be given only at the end of the meal when toasted bread is passed around the table with cheese.

It may well happen that a silent toast is drunk in memory of a deceased person, but it is hardly found that custom *requires* it anywhere. It is an exception: custom wishes much more to "let live"; it allows festivities; as is said in German, it allows *hoch leben,* and the glasses themselves are symbolically lifted up—in fact, at times even the celebrated is lifted up as well.

Eating and drinking customs are not only linked with hospitality. Independently of that, they are related to an expression of common interest and geniality in clubs and fraternities, as students who like to meet every evening to sing *Ergo bibamus* or *Gaudeamus igitur.* But even here the forms of the banquet, at least on festive occasions, are frequently maintained, be it that the president of the club or the elders of the guild do the "honors of the house," or that besides the members there are guests present whom the speaker or senior wishes to make welcome. Such an association, like a good housefather, is assiduous in honoring guests; since custom wills it, it appears natural.

When Aeschylus in the *Eumenides* equates behavior toward guests with behavior toward parents, we find this point of contiguity again. Here, guests as well as parents obtain their rank through custom, and both ranks are analogous to the gods'. But the natural basis of custom differs in these cases. The feeling for parents, and thus also for the deceased ancestors and the gods, is predominantly gratitude bound up with timidity and awe—piety. Such feelings can be shown even to the stranger, if he is an acquaintance or a paternal guest. Hence this behavior can be regarded as a response.

But other motives already referred to are prevalent. The Greeks, in particular, believed that the rejected stranger can be formidable in his curse; and the special sanctity of the right of hospitality is dependent on this belief. To be sure, the *desire to* and the *pride in* being able to help, to accord shelter and board play a role in this, but such benevolence can only be developed among peaceful, friendly peoples who have either dispensed with the more original brutality or who have by nature a nobler predisposition toward others.

As a rule, custom supports and strengthens those dispositions which are tamer, and on the whole more feminine. Custom gives preference to supporting the preserving and peaceful instincts and in the course of human development, so far as this allows the *humane* to grow in men, does so more and more. Custom means domestication; custom means culture. If custom gives sanctuary to the old, to women, to children, to strangers and the poor, then this is a feature common to them all: the fact that it works against brutality, with which it must wage a constant and bitter struggle in all these respects.

And we see how the religious motives are everywhere linked with custom. Indeed, the servants of religion become in the broadest sense the administrators of custom. All too often, however, the brutality of individuals, like the brutality of superstition, is operative in another sense. That is, it sanctifies and upholds barbarian tradition. Thus religion can exert its power to debase as well as to elevate custom. The better customs, like the more humane religions, are characteristic of the leading peoples of mankind. This is true despite the fact that enormous brutalities and barbarisms have remained effective among these same people. Indeed, they have developed while the civilization advanced.

We often find custom and religion working together in praiseworthy amity in the relationships discussed—especially for widows and orphans, for the sick and the wounded, and for misfortunates of all types. Charity, in which custom and religion are combined, even exceeds a healthy measure as it ceases to rest in true *Gemeinschaft*. In this case it demoralizes poverty and reassures the wealthy in their complacency. As almsgiving, it goes along with the harshest egoism and with systematic exploitation practiced in legal forms. It is even being made subservient to such purposes, not to mention that it panders to societal vanity and to aspirations for prestige. It is generally cold and conventional, just as all custom is in danger of becoming so. It handicaps thorough improvement of social conditions guided by scientific insights.

Custom and religion are conservative forces, and as such they often become devoid of understanding, of thought, and of meaning. The interests of authority lie often in preserving ignorance and simple-mindedness, and that is why authority is more concerned about religion than about custom.

Custom is ever directed towards fraternal fellowship, cooperation and mutual aid. Thus the customs of work have an emotional element, which preserves the dignity and honor of labor, as in earlier times the custom of the guilds. Riehl designates with a Hegelian word the four great S's: *Stamm, Sprache, Sitte, Siedelung* (tribe, language, custom, settlement)—the basis of all active life of a people. They form that basis because in them are contained the remnants of the ancient *Gemeinschaft* which often may be found in the modern working-class. As Peter Kropotkin so aptly says, "The core of institutions, customs and usages for mutual aid remains alive in the masses."

❋　　❋　　❋

But as custom depends upon fostering love, friendship and good fellowship, it also gives them their forms—those of mutual honor and delight. Just as usage *facilitates* the behavior of the individual, making it convenient for us and sparing us the trouble of thinking, custom promotes *Gemeinschaft* through these apparently neutral usages. One complies with the form, and thus one does that which may be justifiably expected.

Custom prescribes that in happy *and* sad family events, the neighbors and friends—indeed, also the colleagues and superiors—be notified: one only need act according to custom in order to fulfill their expectations and demands. Older and simpler customs were satisfied with oral messages or letters for the occasion. More and more, the printed or engraved announcement, together with the obligatory acknowledgments has become a universal usage. Here, also, the conventionalization of custom is apparent.

Actually, custom is more faithful to itself where it meets the natural inclination of men to rejoice and be happy with one another. Here it becomes not so easily a "mere form" but demands to do what people following their "heart's desire" like to do (particularly *young* people, such as singing and dancing). Communal singing has become a custom characteristic mostly of the sociability of young men, and communal dancing of men and women. In this latter, the enjoyment and interest are mostly that of the women. Both were at one time predominantly *cult* activities.

Singing survives in our religious usage—particularly congregational singing. Dancing in honor of the gods we know as a primitive usage, and dancing in honor of men is certainly not unfamiliar to us. Monarchs, in order to honor one another, like to give ballets as the festive performances; and one might recall the torch-dances which the Prussian ministers performed at royal weddings.

Hence custom reigns over the entire realm of "good form." This is a subject which has often captured the attention of those interested in human affairs. Indeed this is even more true in more recent times, due to the increasing preoccupation with causal explanations of human behavior in terms of *origins*.

Herbert Spencer, a generation ago,* heralded this type of sociological investigation within the framework of his system of sociology, particularly in the volume *Ceremonial Institutions* which is to derive all manners and polite ceremonies from

* It must be remembered that *Die Sitte* was published in 1909.

specifically devoted to this subject. He attempted behavior of the vanquished and captives, of slaves and subjects. He attempted to explain their forms, which are often so strange, in terms of their origin in actual activities in which content and meaning were not yet differentiated. The famous philosopher amassed numerous data in order to present the development of good form in this way. Yet he overlooks the fact that even where conquest is out of the question, good form can arise, which springs from mutual affection and love and gives expression to these sentiments. Thus it is probably more natural that embraces, kisses and handshakes are understood as immediate expressions of joy in each other and in proximity, than as derived from an originally one-sided homage, which then was partially reciprocated.

It must, however, be conceded that the origin of most of the types of forms of devotedness and salutation which Spencer presents are to be sought in expressions of servility. Hence bowing, the kissing of hands and feet, the sprinkling of parts of the body with sand or ashes, the folding of hands and the uplifting of the folded hands, the baring of head and feet and, in addition to the corresponding forms of speech and particularly of *address*, the flowery phrases which we have, even today, so painstakingly preserved in epistolary style.

Spencer also remarks that in honorific gestures or phrases, the two elements are united, one expressing submission, the other affection. This is in complete agreement with what I have said about the nature of reverence. But he explicitly emphasizes, in regard to phrases, that affirmations of sympathy in the welfare and good fortune of another must have arisen earlier than affirmations of submission.

Whatever the chronological relationship may be, we see clearly that the one and the other "assurances," however earnestly intended they might originally have been, become gradually devoid of substance until they are mere ways of speech or phraseology. They have been demanded of us by custom regardless of whether or not the corresponding sentiment (and, indeed, the corresponding gestures) are behind them. They become mere forms, and only as such can they become a *duty*.

But Spencer traces all these forms and formulae back exclusively to the demeanor of conquered enemies and captives—slaves—toward their conquerors and masters. He does not recognize the fact that in a community of friends who are originally homogeneous, the roots of such customs *also* exist; that the woman is as a rule devoted to serving her husband and also, particularly as a suitor, the man his woman. He does not acknowledge that children, by nature awed, humble and devoted, give reverence to their parents, particularly when they have reached "the age of reason," and that in this is rooted the respect which is rendered to age, the aged *per se*. Above all, he does not perceive how these usages grow out of, and thus remain linked with, the essence of custom.

Indeed, we might say: manners are, as far as their main content is concerned, derived from the nature of *custom* as we have undertaken to trace it back to its form and its concept. "Complaisant behavior" toward older people lies at the basis of all of them. Gift-giving and service are but different expressions of the will contained in this. And this will is first generalized as good will toward the weak ones, in that it is extended to women, children, and guests. Custom wills this because chiefly the old, and then the gods, desire it.

With the young and the strong, the tender inclinations of respect and gratitude and kindred sentiments, and also the enjoyment of physical strength, respond to this. Something resembling condescension inevitably accompanies obliging behavior. And reciprocity is always understood in elementary relationships where only *natural* distinctions apply. Their very diversity brings this about: those who are honored, in turn honor. Even the old are courteous toward women, and women toward the old. Children must honor, but receive no honor; however, they are given things and are cared for. And guests are at another time hosts.

On the other hand, according to their nature, expressions of good will imply reciprocity—so far as good will is gratitude, and love is granted and shown to receive love. Empty forms are not so easily developed in family life and even expressions of submissiveness do not so easily become one-sided. The imperious nature, the strictness and severity of rearing, stem partly from emotions and partly from principles which are foreign to the nature of family life. Seigneurial status belongs only to a widening social life, and here manners become more drastically one-sided: the "obedient servant" on the one side and the "merciful lord," the "gracious lady" (whose displeasure is often cruelly manifested) on the other. In contrast to that, one is his most "informal" among brothers or among comrades; one "lets himself go" or they make no "fuss" with one another.

There is too much similarity for a "stiffness" to arise which is always present on the part of servants and submissives who "await commands," and also on the part of the masters who do not forget themselves and do not wish to make themselves "common." "Society" now reestablishes a kind of equality, in that it favors an *apparent* reciprocity, at least a portion of devotion. Most significant in this respect is the phrase "the pleasure's all mine." At any rate, "empty words" have their widest field here. For the bowing and other flourishes happen to be very different in degree and in involvement, depending upon the occasion. The hat is merely tipped, or it is lowered to the ground. Everyone still feels a bit obligated by custom to humble himself and to exalt others. In the Orient the polite man says, "Everything I have is yours; dispose of my possessions as you please."

Aside from Spencer, who in this regard created a masterwork, manners have been thoroughly analyzed by Jhering in his unfinished *Der Zweck im Recht* mentioned earlier. Jhering notes that language conceives of custom with clarity and certainty as being concerned with the *forms* of activity; the idea would be that of something outward which was added. Closely related to this would be the idea of the *type*, which has developed with regard to manners, as that which has been established. As an example of the proper kind, those of the courts would prevail; beside that, the manner of the town-dweller or possibly that of the knight. Chivalry, which originates in knighthood, is regarded as the proper and helpful demeanor toward women. As all beauty would be dependent upon form, so also would this be true of custom, to which was linked the point of view of aesthetic beauty. In this sense, the word *Anstand* might be characteristic—"bearing" meaning a canon of behavior prescribed by custom. And language would only link such adjectives to the word "demeanor," as are determined by custom.

By the predicates which apply to them, language is observant of the sharp distinction between custom and morality (well-bred and proper in contrast to ethical; honorable and respectable in contrast to honest). The former are referents to something purely external and the latter to something internal. The practical function of feeling was likewise distinguished: conscience in regard to morality, tact in regard to custom, and taste in regard to the beautiful.

Jhering then refers again to manners in his comprehensive *Theorie der Sitte.* For him, the standard of refined custom is three-fold: bearing, courtesy, tact. According to Jhering, all the remaining expressions of which the language makes use belong to one of these three categories, which are circumscribed by these terms.

I believe that Jhering commits a noteworthy *quid pro quo* in this connection. The fact that ideas like decorum, courtesy, and good or refined custom are essentially distinct from the ideas which are contained in the word "custom," completely eludes Jhering, who is otherwise an astute student of language. They all comprise a *judgment,* the latter expressions even more especially. They all establish the idea of what is correct or what should be. This acts as a demand on behavior just as the concepts for morality to which they, in a broader sense, belong.

Nothing like this adheres to the word "custom." We found three ideas related to custom which must be differentiated conceptually. These are the ideas of actual usage, of norm, and of social will. But norm and social will are also thought of as actual, and actual usage is always presumed. Even if custom is at the same time *will,* and even *chiefly* will, it yet ceases to exist when it disappears from practice. The essence of custom *is* practice.

On the other hand, ideas like bearing and courtesy are purely theoretical. They are *ideal* standards against which actual conduct is measured. They contain rules of a character which is half aesthetic and half ethical; the value and validity of these rules are thought to be *independent* of whether or not they are actually observed and followed. They may very often concur with and coincide with the norms of custom. This is particularly true because they are derived from custom.

Custom is the predominant basis of valid points of view—viewpoints about what is decorous, proper, courteous, and so on. But these views can also emancipate themselves from custom and contradict it. Very often something that custom has not only licensed but even supports and commands is found to be indecent, indeed shocking, by the sensitive.

Only consider wedding customs. Custom and the views which rest within it—views regarding decency, demeanor and "way of life"—belong essentially to rural life. Custom, as folk-custom, is the indigenous, the traditional, the common. This is true of the forms of social intercourse as well. Here are far-reaching equality, simplicity, naiveté, and therefore warmth and heartiness. But here also are virile native roughness and coarseness, although the development of "manners" or "deportment" is certainly not alien among peasants. Indeed the latter are even asserted in sharply defined judgments and precepts, particularly at the important events in life. Here it is actual custom which binds and commands.

However, the views of the upper and ruling classes and those of the urbanites are formed outside of custom (although mostly *out* of custom). These views partially originate in deviant new usages and habits, and the latter are frequently based on an imitation of strangers. New, special "customs" are also formed, but they are always intended to ennoble and to refine the original, older custom. The refined way of life, so characteristic of civilization, in which, as Kant says, men are one and all actors, is called "courtesy."

This nomenclature is due to its usage in the houses of princes and people of rank. But in other languages it is called *civilité*, civility and urban behavior—urbaneness. In every case, it is a sign of culture and education ever of more recent origin, and *not* a sign of "old" custom. In the appreciation of those, the aesthetic viewpoint tends to prevail. The affected elegance of the man of the world is preferred to the natural bluntness of the rustic, polish is preferred to "rough" manners, and a smooth to a coarse exterior.

The ideas of decorum and courtesy are not, as Jhering maintains, on the same level. The first is the more comprehensive of the two. To be courteous and amenable belongs to decorum. By "decorum" one thinks generally of that which is becoming to the person, and a courteous manner toward others is part of it. In the concept of courtesy, the value which it may have for ourselves is not considered, but only the effect it has on *others* and the value it may have for them.

Jhering makes a fine distinction between self-advantageous customs and customs which are advantageous for others. However, he studies forms of social intercourse exclusively from the point of view of how they are useful to others.

As already noted, the aesthetic point of view prevails in the estimation of decorum and courtesy. However, that is not to say that the ethical point of view is strange to it. Coarseness is interpreted as hostility, and it exists mainly in that unfriendly feelings are manifested in a candid, *i.e.*, rough manner. On the other hand, urbaneness and courtesy—*refined* custom—demand that some consideration be given (to others), and that if such feelings are sustained toward another, they are at least not flaunted.

Refined custom demands a certain measure of friendliness even toward the enemy and toward the unsympathetic. Certainly the moral sense which demands sincerity rebels against this. The courtier who says something pleasing to everyone is reputed to be false; one wonders that he can smile and always smile and still be a knave. But the necessity for sociability and peaceful communication, which if it is not stronger, is at least more pervasive in the upper classes and in urban strata, is decisive in favor of pleasant falseness. This would certainly be innocuous if really, as Kant thinks, no one would be deceived by it "because everyone knows what he should take it for"—flourishes and all the fawning gallantries, together with the most ardent protestations of friendship and high esteem.

However, that is only *partially* true (although perhaps to the *greater* part). A margin always remains in which deception has broad room for play. The inexperienced—particularly women—are the most easily deluded. But often it is also difficult, indeed impossible, for the experienced to distinguish between the sincere compliment and mere phrases, or between recognition and flattery. It is precisely this uncertainty which makes flattery and everything related to it such a dangerous instrument in the hands of those who wish to obtain something by it. As a rule, flattery is the poison of princes, whether or not (or even precisely because) sincerity so easily becomes an offense against them.

Urban or court manners are often imitated. What is refined is always admired as superior. Thus the usages of people in the cities and people of rank pervade those of the country-folk and the lower strata of the population. Hence what was once a mark of distinction can become common custom, and this is rather frequently the case. Ever and anon this process is repeated: the wealthy and those of rank distinguish themselves from general custom even when they themselves originally borrowed it. And ever and anon they seek to differentiate themselves, to erect a wall between themselves and the "common rabble."

This tendency can lead to the strangest, the most absurd customs, such as the binding of the young girl's feet in old China. Jhering calls it the body's protest against the suspicion that its bearer belongs to the lower classes, since only those Chinese who can afford to be carried about in a sedan-chair are supposed to allow themselves this luxury. But this pragmatic explanation hardly clarifies the origin of the custom.

The tendencies toward equality are notorious in contemporary Europe. Imitation has an enormously rapid pace. To be sure, in most things only the outward appearance can be obtained, and it is always easy to present the genuine and the authentic as the prerogative of the ruling classes. But appearances deceive, and only the superficial strikes the eye. Hence it is always difficult to distinguish oneself. If imitation has become indiscriminate ostentation, then the distinguished can be discerned by their *simplicity*. This is most readily manifested in clothing, and we have already discussed clothing as a very important object of custom in general. Clothing serves the inclination to appear distinguished, and it serves the rules of decorum as well.

❊   ❊   ❊

The clothing of genuine custom as it exists among country-folk is the national dress or "costume." The more distinguished attire of the great, like that of city people, is different from this. It becomes a preferred symbol of class and rank. As such it continues to remain subject to custom, although according to its nature it is a matter of social beliefs and tastes. The belief is that certain clothing is appropriate *per se*—for example, that the black color is suitable and correct for the clergy, as for mourning (black and white compete in both cases), while in contrast perhaps purple is appropriate for the imposing dignity of chiefs and princes.

But at the courts costume becomes the object of special, express precepts which determine and regulate the costume as if they were laws. The uniform is demanded earliest in military service. There clothing, particularly while on duty, is subject to regulations. Indeed, it is subject to law. Here all individuality expressed through clothing disappears. This is a tendency which is a fulfillment of that already existing in the simple folk-costume.

On the other hand, the desire for distinction brings about ever-new changes of dress and ornamentation. This is chiefly the case in cities, and all the more so as wealth spreads in them. The frequent change of dress serves to document wealth as well as taste. As one changes in the course of the day, so also one changes according to seasons and from year to year. A new regime asserts itself:

the regime of fashion. This is most striking in feminine dress, to which the term "fashion" specifically refers.

Fashion somewhat resembles custom. Both expressions are often used interchangeably and are confused. But their objects differ widely, although they are not mutually exclusive artificially *or* conceptually. Good or refined custom, in those very aspects that *are* custom, borders closely on fashion and easily crosses over into it. This is because it is more dependent upon ephemeral tastes and novel experiences than is genuine custom, which renders the traditional pattern rigidly and constantly. Fashion, too, is a form of social will. But while custom precedes the judgment that is the taste of opinion, fashion characteristically follows these types of sentiment and thought.

The notion that something, in order to be noticed and pleasing, must be new and strange or different is of the essence of fashion. Also, fashion consists of the notion that the newest thing must always be interesting—at least for the curious—and that men, too, therefore, who want to be noticed and to be pleasing, must *appear* ever new and impeccably dressed (for it is impossible to *be* always new and impeccably dressed). This appearance is possible if one possesses new things and exhibits them. But their newness is the more apparent the more the "cut" is new and striking. And this is most easily visible in clothing, particularly in the splendid garments of women which strike the eye of society.

The authoritative images of the few are imitated by the many. The fact that they often are imitated by the *demi-monde,* and that business interests lurk behind them, is little known and quickly forgotten. Soon "everyone" agrees that one *must* be clothed in such-and-such a manner, if one wants to show that one "belongs." Fashion is "conventional" by nature. It originates as if it were made by the conscious choice of the pace-setting personalities of the "upper 10,000" and indeed chiefly for the purpose of establishing a model, of making known one's own arbitrariness or capacity to "set the tone" in order to denote *the* society.

Jhering excellently states, "Fashion is the incessantly rebuilt barrier by which high society takes pains to shut itself off from the middle stratum in society." (The danger of being confused with the lowest stratum, he states earlier, does not have to be considered, since it is excluded as a matter of course.) "It is the race of vanity between classes, wherein one and the same phenomenon is repeated: the endeavor of one group to obtain an advantage, no matter how small, in differentiating themselves from their imitators; and the other group's endeavor to equalize that advantage through immediate adaptation of the new fashion."

Custom and fashion must be strictly distinct from one another. However, they have much in common; they have several similar traits. Fashion, too, is social will. It has an active role in behavior. "If everyone does it, I also must do it. I must follow the fashion." This is the reasoning of every woman who considers herself "in society" or "upper class," particularly concerning the fashion in which she has her dresses made. Through this reasoning she recognizes an unwritten precept to be valid for her. She submits herself to the compulsion of fashion. And how is this compulsion exerted? Through the criticism which one invites whenever one appears in public: public opinion. One becomes the slave of fashion; one follows its whims blindly. We always say "one" or "everyone." Women are the essential elements in this, and when we speak of "women" we also refer to the feminine in the male as indicative of the "dandy."

Thus fashion, like custom, invades every province

of life. It is custom-become-fluid; hence it is custom-become-casual and superficial. Therefore it is custom which has become perverted into its contrary. For it is the nature of custom to be archaic, fixed, heavy and serious. According to J. von Falke, it was in about the middle of the fourteenth century that first occurred what we since that time understand by "fashion"—the "eternal, apparently chance change in costume, with its absolute rule over all classes of civilized humanity which had triumphed over mere existence and the simple perpetuation of life . . . ; documents give certain proof of how people at that time became conscious of fashion as a power."

One can also denote fashion as the custom of the young—not so much younger *ages* as younger social strata. Above all, fashion is the custom of the inhabitants of large cities where industries which serve and live from fashion develop with alacrity. Custom develops in *time,* and hence in many vertical lines, from the bottom up so to speak. Fashion spreads in space. Custom tends to become particular, and fashion to become general.

Jhering noted barely *en passant* that manners are also to a large degree dependent upon fashion. Manners are "dictated" by fashion, because the *good* society shows them off in order to indicate its "re-finement," although the need for producing something new finds little room in this case. Here the stable element is naturally stronger than in the case of clothing. This stable element has its locus where custom is based on natural understanding. And this is actually traceable to honor, which is rendered to the elders and to women, and generally to natural distinctions, although fashion (as if intentionally) often ignores these.

Partly, too, it is yet a genuine custom about which one does not think, or perhaps of which one is not even cognizant. Thus we have the German custom of the handshake after a festive dinner, accompanied by the words *Gesegnete Mahlzeit* (and often the *Gesegnete*, which is actually the point, is omitted.) These words are almost spoken mechanically. One is hardly conscious of an express *wish*, let alone the older meaning of the words which signifies the communal enjoyment of a cult ritual resembling the Christian communion.

Recently it has become the "fashion" to kiss a lady's hand at this and other occasions. As is known, hand-kissing, as the kissing of the hem of a garment, is a national custom even today, in those areas where the people are kept in a position of servility and submission. The Catholics kiss the hand of the priests. And to kiss ladies' hands, particularly elderly ones', is likewise an old, chivalrous custom which has survived in the families and circles of nobility. Nevertheless, I call this habit which has recently been diffused, "mere" fashion. This is because it is based upon exterior imitation and upon the attraction novelty has for bourgeois circles. It lacks the tradition and piety which characterize the observance of *custom*. Here, as everywhere, fashion is charged with a sense of what is elegant, flattering, and highly flexible.

The primary reason for imitation is purely social —that is, to show that one knows what is proper, to manifest oneself as a *cavalier à la mode* (as the phrase went 200 years ago), although the individual is not always aware of these motives. If a fashion becomes a common thing, then it is soon discovered that it *is* common and one then desires to be differentiated from it, to show that one does not go along with it. Simmel comments on fashion in a witty way, saying that its peculiarly piquant and stimulating charm consists in the contrast between its breadth of pervasiveness which leaves no one untouched, and its quick and thorough ephemerality, its prerogative for perfidy.

One must also determine whether fashion is
merely a usage or is grounded in a norm or law
or a power indicating a law-giving will. This is
the real meaning in which we discuss fashion here.
But different *types* of will, contained in custom as
well as fashion, must again be distinguished. That
which custom allows was already discussed; fashion, too, allows many a thing without formally ap-
proving or recommending it. It suffices for them
that they show themselves as *master*. And every
master makes his will known in many gradations.
He permits many things; he advises and favors and
recommends many others. Others he tries to check
by disapproval, censure and admonition. Only to
that which he deems important does he refer with
more or less strict command and prohibition; a rec-
ommendation gradually becomes an order.

As often as it is decried as tyrannical, however,
fashion is not strict by nature; it is too inconstant
for that. Where it commands in a strict manner,
there it is also lasting and absorbs an ideal content.
It is called good or genteel custom. Thus it is
prescribed that men wear white tie and tails for
formal dinners and many other occasions. And
again, in such things the prescriptions of societal
custom must be distinguished from the commands

of "propriety." He who appears at a banquet in a simple frock coat violates custom but not propriety, provided the coat is "proper." But if several buttons are torn off and grease spots are visible, this will be "no longer respectable." But he who appears in a clown's costume—elegant as it may be—suffers the comment that he oversteps the limits of tact and good taste; he will be rebuked as silly. And if one arrives late and takes his place at the host's table without "paying his compliments" to the host or other guests at the *table d'hôte,* we say that he ignores the law of hospitality or decency.

We have already drawn attention to the difference between these "codes" and custom. Certainly custom too deems that one don "festive garments" for festive occasions. This rule is not only confined to "polite society." But, where it is truly alive, custom is regularly and conscientiously obeyed, and he who deviates from it appears almost deranged. This indicates how absolutely necessary custom considers itself.

On the other hand, genteel custom is set up as an ideal. It is considered an art to conduct oneself "impeccably" in relation to its demands. It requires study into which one must be introduced, and in the highest circles the master of ceremonies alone knows everything which enters into it. "Etiquette" is the rule here (as it is called according to the labels which referred to everyone by his rank and thus his place and seat). Etiquette is neither custom nor fashion. Like custom it is severe and rigid; like fashion it is superficial and lacks roots in the folkways. It is soulless custom.

By virtue of its ceremonies and rituals, genteel custom is akin to religion from which, on the other hand, it is entirely different because genteel custom is essentially worldly and primarily serves pleasure. But the points of contact are the formalities and ceremonies. Hence every case which concerns a cult has both elements. In this sense the cult of the dead comes to mind and, too, the almost wholly religious cult which customarily is due the "majesties."

Finally there is the cult which men have, as of old, devoted to women. In this case particularly we note custom in transition to *genteel* custom, in its refinement and chivalrous effect. But it becomes idle vanity and a luxurious gentility as well, where a glittering exterior hides the decay, as has always been the case at the courts and in too many salons. Fashion is always a phase and a symptom of the dissolution of custom. This is the case precisely because fashion neither wills to be nor *can* be popular, but rather is privileged, distinguished and distinguishing. For that reason, the poet wishes that joy may again unite *"was die Mode streng geteilt"* ("that which fashion has strictly divided").

The customs of aristocracy and other "estates," if they are genuine customs at all, have this in common with fashion. Thus we have the highly characteristic custom of dueling. Jhering refers to the duel as a type of evil custom or "abuse." However, this does not contribute to an understanding of the nature of dueling. Dueling denotes the aristocracy, and particularly the estate of warriors and knights whose honor is almost solely based upon valor. It expresses the autonomy of this status group which claims to settle controversies or "quarrels" within its own ranks, according to its own custom—*i.e.*, according to its own will and the rules contained therein.

It is contrary to the nature of the modern state, which in principle recognizes no status group that is exempt from its laws and makes exceptions only in favor of the high nobility. Therefore, it ought to be repressed with particular severity by this state. However, it is precisely the class which practices this custom which possesses enough influence (at least in some states) to establish and maintain a lenient, special law which, although prohibiting dueling and placing it under penalty, actually favors it.

Any custom of a status group shares a feature of fashion, insofar as it does not intend to be popular and common. Thus the custom of dueling is also imitated by those who, though not belonging to such a distinguished status, at least want to emulate it in this one particular point. The attraction, particularly for younger men, is so strong that it outweighs the danger to life and limb. This is true whether that attraction exists through a sense of honor or through vanity. Hence whole groups which aspire to belong to the aristocracy have appropriated a custom like that of dueling. To be sure, the fear of being conspicuous and stigmatized as a man who does *not* belong, and consequently who is not a "man of honor," may be even stronger than the attraction for dueling itself.

The ruling classes of a society always play a dual role which is often divided among different strata of the class. On the one hand, they start innovations, insofar as they often import "new fashions" from foreign countries. On the other hand, they are staunchly conservative and strongly "nationalistic." Thus they adhere to the old customs precisely because their own position is based on age. Nobility is always typical of both, and indeed it is not seldom that a younger nobility ("paper barons") represents the one role and the older nobility the other role, or at least accentuates it more. But the latter, conservative though it may be, behaves differently depending upon the object and purpose.

Due to the close unity between custom and religion, custom as religious custom remains especially popular, universal, and at the same time durable. Religious custom, it is true, has suffered a severe rupture in the German countries due to the schism in the church. At the time of the Restoration, the nobility sought its support in religious custom all the more, as it now constituted itself as authority over against the commoners. Through the privilege of patronage it could also hold the religious congregation in tutelage.

But assiduous as it was—particularly in the throes of the seventeenth century—to distinguish its status more sharply from the people, the nobility refused to share in religious custom. It appeared "disreputable for a noble child to be baptized with the same water as that used to baptize common children." One introduced private baptisms and private confirmations. One requested of the sovereign that he take the "holy supper" at home or in church before (instead of after) the worship. Two noble ladies complained in a petition to the Elector of Saxony that at communion they "had to elbow their way through the great masses of common people with many inconveniences and annoyances." One no longer wants to "commune with" the great masses. Soon the nobility no longer required that the banns be proclaimed, nor the wedding performed in church.

Even the funeral customs were changed (all, according to Paul Drews, "Der Einfluss der gesellschaftlichen Zustände auf das kirchliche Leben," *Zeitschrift für Theologie und Kirche* XVI, I). The nobility preferred quiet burials at night by torchlight with elaborate funeral orations, instead of the customary sermon. The nobility shunned ecclesiastical discipline. At sacred rituals they even disregarded the traditional solemn and strict customary attention, conversing "as if they were at a ball or an opera or even a banquet." (Drews, *op. cit.*)

It is also interesting how pietism, which essentially worked in the opposite or popular direction, was adopted by the nobility in order "to have it appear that what was illegal as social privilege is now legal and justifiable as a means of edification." For public church ceremonies could be scorned as "unedifying" in the sense of a pietistic way of thinking. In this regard, pietism has paved the way for rationalism.

For rationalism the significance of ecclesiastical forms and religious procedures generally wanes. It substitutes a fashionable intellectuality which is necessarily exclusive for simple, childlike beliefs rooted in tradition. Education, when it is scientific, undermines religion more than custom. It is specifically the genteel or good custom, particularly with the assistance of state power, which can preserve or restore religious custom. However, religious custom thereby easily becomes hypocritical and mendacious, thus losing everything of internal beauty which it ever possessed.

❖   ❖   ❖

Society, as the subject and supporter of fashion,

stands in a certain contrast to custom. It is modern, cultured, cosmopolitan. It represents new principles throughout; it desires progress. Trade, the production of goods—the workshop, and the factory —are the elements by which it extends its network over the whole populated earth. It desires movement and *quick* movement; it must dissolve custom in order to develop a taste for the new and for imported goods. It figures on individual motives, especially on young people's curiosity and love of finery, and on the desire to barter and to trade in desired goods. Affection and fidelity to tradition, to one's own, to one's heritage, must necessarily give way. Commerce has ever a disintegrating effect.

Trade and commerce, urban life, the growth of big cities, the power of money, capitalism, class differentiation, and the striving for middle-class status and education—all these are facets of the same development of civilization, which favors fashion and is injurious to custom. Even the country folk soon find their old customs peculiar and absurd. Cheap, glittering wares impress them more than the old-fashioned household wares with the beautiful if quaint designs. And so it is in everything. The pattern of the metropolis is imitated.

Goods quickly manufactured with mechanized techniques are often ugly and not durable, like the fashion from which they spring. All *gesellschaftliche* civilization has a quality utterly opposed to the artistic spirit which is rooted in tradition and in integrity. It is superficial and external. The items of mass production are flimsy, uniform, monotonous; they lack genuineness.

Thus an age in which fashion and *gesellschaftliche* civilization predominate becomes powerful over against an age which underlies it and is yet retained within it: an age in which custom predominates, as an age of peasant-townsmen culture and the culture of the clergy and the nobility resting upon it. The former is pervaded with haste, unrest, continual novelty, fluidity and a persistence only in incessant change. Hence it is inclined to idealize its opposite; the antique becomes the style. One longs to return to nature; old castoffs are resurrected; old forms of life and old customs are valued and preserved.

A taste for religion is reactivated, and the simplicity, the homespun nature of genuine style and artistically correct forms are "discovered." This cycle recurs in rhythmic waves from time to time. Industry capitalizes on this fashion as it does on others. The spirit of *Gesellschaft* remains the same: it cannot jump over its own shadow. But in its forward movement lies the possibility of surmounting it. This lies in the reorganization of the economic foundations. If the natural interchange of production and consumption were to replace the predominance of the movable capital of trade and commerce, then, too, life would again become more stable, more quiet and more healthy. Consciously-nurtured custom and the fostering of art would again be possible.

Even religion would find new life as a *Weltanschauung* in the spirit of truth; or better, the idea of religion would be re-awakened in the struggle for the spirit of truth and reverence. A society that unanimously pursues such a course, and with a clear and strong consciousness, would manifest an abandonment of the whims of fashion and an ability to produce a rational will. The growth of its rationality is that which in general distinguishes it. It is that which lies in the developmental lines of custom and civilization, and as such in its ennoblement and refinement.

These developmental lines have been repeatedly stressed: emancipation from superstition, spiritism and magic, the joy in intellectual pursuit, which itself can become an appreciation of art, and a striving for artistic naiveté and creativity. The present contains such elements and moments, although only in the form of a few scattered grains of seed. It can rather be said that the future *ought to be* developed in such a direction than that it *will* be.

The state, too, in its empirical appearance the other expression of society, exerts an effect on custom wholly analogous to that which society exerts on it. Custom is concrete, particularizing, rural, provincial-urban. The state represents an individual-abstract will which regulates—that is, wills to establish uniformity. Through ordinances and laws it fights custom where it seems noxious or only dangerous to it. The esteem of custom is diminished everywhere due to the state's absolute authority. The state serves progress, the development of independent personalities, but always at the expense of the folk and their *gemeinschaftlich* cooperative life.

It is futile, as many thinkers and scholars might be tempted to do, to lament this. The more one understands the inner necessity of the process, the more his lament will be silenced. But he does not need to suppress a sense of the tragic in the course of things. Precisely because the progress is so immense, the collapse of tradition is highly charged with emotion. For the expectation that progress will restore or reestablish the good of the old life is linked with progress itself; and this it is not able to do. It can only achieve its own objective. It gives men the opportunity of livelihood and, in what time is left, the opportunity for education as well.

Everything native, genial and homely disappears. The individual is thrown on his own resources. In the name of economic progress and rational agriculture, the state promotes the dissolution of the genuine village-community, the partitioning of pasture held in common, the abolishment of *Gemengelage** and *Flurzwang†*—all of which was regulated by custom.

Like the life and law of the peasants, so was that of the townsmen, especially that of the artisan in his guild and town, ruled by custom which, in turn, was based on the idea of natural concord and brotherhood. The spirit of custom is commu-

---

* Pattern of fields developed when the land owned by each farmer consists of a number of small, widely scattered plots.

† Obligation of all villagers to carry on uniform sowing, tilling, harvesting, etc. of their fields.

nistic, and so it remains despite the development of private property. Within custom, individual rights are not stark and absolute; they are directed toward rather than against each other.

Only a technically developed, national law like that of the Romans, or state legislation which absorbs it or is erected on the same principles, place individual rights in the foreground. They know nothing but individuals and government, the latter preferably conceived of as an individual also. These individuals are partially organized in their relationships to each other through law, and partially through a free contract. Law becomes distinct from morality to which custom had bound it. According to this notion, everyone is a potential enemy, or at least a litigant, because everyone wishes to get something from everyone else, although through legal devices. Custom and religion are a highly imperfect, often childlike and sometimes child*ish* expression of the folk spirit, but they *are* the people's own will, in which it rejoices.

The will of *authority*, on the other hand, although it can be theoretically construed as one established or authorized by the people, confronts it as a strange will. This shows most strikingly in the period of absolute monarchy, which still survives in constitutional form. "The characteristic of this concept (of authority) is that the state is regarded as something apart from the people; that it concentrates in the abstract concept of the state the sum total of public power; that authority is the visible representation of this abstract concept but that besides the state only individuals exist." (Gierke.)

"While the communal constitution determines the organization, by means of which the community rules itself, the authoritarian constitution contains the organization by which the community *is being* ruled. . . . If the authoritarian principle thus aspires to the realization of the absolute state, then it will at the same time appear as a police state." (*Ibid.*)

The police turn out to be exceedingly useful, indeed necessary, but they are a check on the "public," the subjects, even where they can still move freely under custom. They wish to keep the people apart in order to avert violence. But they also keep them apart where their convening both signifies and promotes harmony, and where it establishes and maintains custom. Here we find everywhere "the territorial disputes between custom and law." How many a well devised usage falls victim to the police's overscrupulousness.

"How many an originally innocent and protective liberty is forbidden by the tutelage of the law, which only brings the danger of abuse to awareness thereby. How often does a government regulation, which appears to be born from arbitrary lust for power, provoke violation which is then no longer innocuous, particularly when one is anxious to outwit nature as well as the authorities. The development of the individual according to his peculiar inclinations and talents is no longer tolerated by bureaucratic uniformity, and every strip of land which in the process of such border regulations is conquered by the incessantly advancing law must be ceded by custom." (Bahnsen, *Der Widerspruch in Wissen und Wesen der Welt*, II, S. 292.)

Schiller praises custom because it makes man free and powerful. Where the police and their state act according to their own intentions, men become enslaved and impotent. They are guarded as if they were children. A people which is in the process of becoming spiritually more mature and stronger will again want to be its own master. It wants to recognize its own identity in the state, and to form itself into the state. It wants to again be self-ruling in the smaller groups.

To the extent that a people succeed in this, a kind of renaissance of custom is possible. This will hold so long as society and the spirit of the time do not oppose it, so long as the freedom acquired and maintained by the ruling classes for their own purposes is not used in society and state to suppress the freedom of the people—that is the masses—who are contrasted to those as the lower classes. In these, the nature of the people with their inclination toward concord and custom —toward "solidarity"—is more strongly preserved. But in their progressing liberation and development, they definitely participate in scientific reasoning which always strengthens the most, and the most directly, tendencies toward individualization.

"La coutume est la raison des sots"—thus did the King of the Enlightenment speak his verdict. In general, the attitude of science toward custom corresponds to this. Science is essentially rationalistic. The great significance of critical philosophy consists in conveying an awareness of this to science, and that it makes it aware of its limitations as well. The most significant limitation is that it

can only imperfectly hold the living to its formulas. The precise account is inadequate if applied to organic facts.

The rationalist attempts to understand and interpret the facts of life mechanistically, and in similar manner the facts of the spirit intellectually. He sees in it more or less wisdom and logical understanding which perceives and constitutes what is useful and expedient. Habit as well as instinct appear to it as something animalistic and obscure, trifling and base. This applies also to custom, which is so often related to superstition, and which is regarded as if it were only that. But this is an inadequate judgment. The thinking person must recognize the unconscious creativity in the human, social and individual spirit, and must find rationality not only in what is rational in *its* form. He will then do justice to habit and custom and to the extremely important function which they eternally fulfill in an individual and a social sense.

Both habit and custom spare labor of the will, insofar as what they regulate functions automatically, removed from doubt and reflection. Thus they simplify life. If only they do not captivate reason, there remains all the more playing-room for its free activity. This convenience is also offered by a system of thought and opinion as religion represents it, together with the prescriptions for action derived therefrom.

These prescriptions regularly harmonize with those of custom, as we found religious custom to be universal. But here, too, conflict is most obviously unavoidable. A faith claims to be, if not established, at least true; therefore it is ever confronted with the forum of scientific thinking. Neither its usefulness nor its value can protect it in this respect.

Custom does not make that claim. But neither does it wish to be judged merely in terms of its expediency: here it would be easily surpassed by rational institutions. It has its worth as good custom and beautiful custom. As good (moral) custom it has ethical worth; as beautiful custom its worth is aesthetic.

Perfect morality has also an aesthetic value and perfect aesthetics has a moral value as well. Both values transcend mere expediency; they have their own rationale. Scientific (discursive) reason cannot therefore imitate that. It can merely perceive and describe it. Nevertheless it will always be opposed to it, because its object is expediency; and, indeed, because it is associated with another taste which is often quickly renovated and thus always changing. This is because the elements of the mind are not independent of one another, but *taste* is an expression of will.

The will which chooses and exhibits expediency is rational will (*Kürwille*). But this association is not necessary and essential. Scientific thought can also be united with natural will (*Wesenwille*) and with the taste which is at its core. It will be inclined toward that, the more profoundly it grasps the facts of organic life and creativity; in other words, the more it grasps the workshop of moral and artistic genius. Thus, too, will the freest thinking recognize, acknowledge and favor in myriad ways the morality of custom. Thus it will be said: Rather an imperfect custom than no custom at all!

In 1881, Nietzsche maintained as a basic insight into the origin of morality—that morality is nothing else but (also nothing more than) obedience to customs of whichever type these may be. The free man, he maintains, is amoral because he wishes to depend on himself in everything rather than on tradition—as if he could not comprehend and honor his heritage as meaningful, beautiful and good, and obey himself by obeying it. The amoralist quite correctly says, in conclusion to this aphorism (*The*

Dawn of Day, 9): "Under the dominating influence of the morality of custom, originality of every kind came to acquire a bad conscience; and even now the sky of the best minds seems to be more overcast by this thought than it need be."*

Indeed, the morality of custom has long since become inadequate. It must be purified in the fire of criticism and it needs—however much of it may prove to be pure gold—supplementation, like the genuine metal requires paper money. A new lawbook of morality which does not hold itself bound to custom has thus become necessary. The more liberated we become *from* custom and become free *within* custom, the more we will need a conscious ethic—that is, the recognition of that which makes man human and the self-affirmation of reason. And reason, precisely through this, must cease being merely a scientific, analytical power. Rather it must develop into the joyous creation of *Gemeinschaft*. It is chiefly by this means that reason will prove to be the "height of human potential"; or, rather, it will only then become it.

* Translation by J. M. Kennedy in *The Dawn of Day*, Oscar Levy, editor (New York: The Macmillan Company, 1924), p. 17.

Biographical Notes

JOHANN JAKOB BACHOFEN (1815-1887)

Bachofen was a Swiss anthropologist and cultural historian. He studied law and legal history at Basel, Berlin (where he came under the influence of Savigny), Oxford, Cambridge, and Paris. When he returned to Basel, he was appointed to the chair of Roman law at the university, but resigned in 1844 to devote himself to the history of art. He later accepted a judgeship in the criminal court at Basel, and held this position until 1877. His best-known work is *Das Mutterrecht: eine Untersuchung über die Gynaikokratie der alten Welt nach ihrer religiösen und rechtlichen Natur* (Stuttgart, 1861; second edition, 1897.)

SOURCE: Heinrich Cunow, "Bachofen," *Encyclopaedia of the Social Sciences*

JULIUS FRIEDRICH AUGUST BAHNSEN (1830-1881)

A philosopher who began his studies of Philology and Philosophy in 1848 at the University of Kiel, Bahnsen was a *Gymnasiallehrer* (a secondary school teacher) in Lauenburg (Pommern). His works include *Zum Verhältnis zwischen Wille und Motiv,* 1870; *Zur Philosophie der Geschichte* (1871); and *Der Widerspruch im Wissen und Wesen der Welt,* 2 vols., to which Tönnies refers in this book.

SOURCE: August Vetter, *Neue Deutsche Biographie*

PAUL DREWS (1858-1912)

A theologian, Paul Drews was a Professor of Evangelical Theology at the University of Halle. His works include *Der evangelische Geistliche in der Deutschen Vergangenheit* (1905) and *Der Einfluss der Gesellschaftlichen Zustände auf das kirchliche Leben* (1906).

SOURCE: *Der Grosse Brockhaus*

JAKOB VON FALKE (1825-1897)

Jakob von Falke was an artist and art historian and served in 1855 as Curator of the German Museum in Nuremberg, in 1858 as Librarian and Director of the Gallery of Prince Liechtenstein in Vienna, and after 1885 as Director of the Austrian Museum for Art and Industry. Among his works are *Die deutsche Trachten- und Modenwelt* (1858; 2 volumes); *Geschichte des modernen Geschmacks* (1866); and *Kostümgeschichte der Kulturvölker* (1882), and several historical volumes on taste and art in handicraft.

SOURCE: *Der Grosse Brockhaus*

Custom: An Essay on Social Codes

OTTO VON GIERKE (1844-1921)

Among the monumental works of this well-known German jurist is the four-volume *Das deutsche Genossenschaftsrecht* (1868, 1873, 1881, and 1913.)

SOURCE: Carl Joachim Friedrich, "von Gierke," *Encyclopaedia of the Social Sciences*

RUDOLF HIRZEL (1846-1917)

Hirzel, a Professor of Classical Philology at Jena, was the author of various studies dealing with problems of ancient law.

SOURCE: *Der Grosse Brockhaus*

RUDOLF VON JHERING (1818-1892)

Rudolf von Jhering was a German jurist and a professor at the universities of Basel, Rostock, Kiel, Giessen, Vienna, and Göttingen successively. "He began his career as a Romanist but developed into the most encyclopaedic mind in German law in the nineteenth century." His most important work (and the work to which Tönnies repeatedly refers) is *Der Zweck im Recht*, 2 volumes (1877-1883). Jhering is the author of numerous other works, among them the three-volume *Der Geist des römischen rechts auf den verschiedenen Stufen seiner Entwicklung* (1852-1865).

SOURCE: J. Wilhelm Hedemann, "von Jhering," *Encyclopaedia of the Social Sciences*

Custom: An Essay on Social Codes

BURKARD WILHELM LEIST (1819-1906)

A German jurist, Leist was successively a professor at the universities of Basel, Rostock, and Jena, where he died. He is the author of several volumes, including *Alt arisches jus gentium* (1889) and the two-volume study, *Alt arisches jus civile* (1892-1896).

SOURCE: Hans Fehr, "Leist," *Encyclopaedia of the Social Sciences*

JUSTUS MÖSER (1720-1794)

Justus Möser was a German man of letters and historian, as well as one of the fathers of the historical school of law, economics, and ethnology. His *Patriotische Phantasien* (four volumes) appeared in Berlin in the years 1774-1786.

SOURCE: K. Brandi, "Möser," *Encyclopedia of the Social Sciences*

WILHELM HEINRICH RIEHL (1823-1897)

A German historian and sociologist, Riehl began his career as a journalist, but was appointed professor at the University of Munich in 1854, first to teach political science and, in 1859, to teach *Kulturgeschichte.* "By virtue of his studies of German society in the middle of the nineteenth century, based on personal observations and a thorough study of the family, Riehl must be considered, along with Lorenz von Stein, as the founder of sociology in Germany." Among Riehl's chief works is *Die Naturgeschichte des Volkes als Grundlage einer deutschen Sozial-Politik,* four volumes, 1851-1864.

SOURCE: Walter Goetz, "Reihl," *Encyclopaedia of the Social Sciences*

GUSTAV VON SCHMOLLER (1838-1917)

Schmoller was an eminent German economist and head of the influential "historical school of Economics." Readers are referred to the source listed below for a complete discussion of his activities and publications.

SOURCE: Hans Gehrig, "Schmoller," *Encyclopaedia of the Social Sciences*